To Rusty & Cookie

As you read, may your wonder grow...

Helen Hunter

(210) 240-6673

THE
JESUS
DIARIES

THE JESUS DIARIES

By
Helen Hunter

The Jesus Diaries
Copyright ©2015 by Helen Hunter. All rights reserved.
Printed in the United States of America.

No part of this publication may be reproduced, stored in a retrieval system, or transmitted by any means—electronic, mechanical, photocopy, recording, or otherwise—without the prior permission of the copyright holder, except as provided by USA copyright law.

The book, *The Jesus Diaries,* is based on the four canonical Gospels of Matthew, Mark, Luke and John in the New Testament of the Bible. Unless otherwise noted, all scriptures are taken from the King James Version of the Bible.

ISBN 13: 978-1519456755 (Print)
ISBN 10: 1519456751

ACKNOWLEDGEMENTS

My most profound thanks go to the following people for their generous help with this manuscript:

James Adair
Valmarie Brown
Paul Drexel
Ruby Grant
Charles Menear
Mary Dan Menear
Elaine Miller
Kevin Reimers
Lizzie Smiley
Khina Subedi
Jeana Watts
Dolores Woodrum

FOREWORD

The Jesus Diaries is a fresh look at a time-honored story told through the eyes of Jesus as the main character. It is a faithful modernization of the essential Gospel story as it is told in the four canonical Gospels of Matthew, Mark, Luke and John.

It tells the story of Jesus in a way that will speak both to long-time believers and to others who are interested in hearing the Gospel story for the first time. I like it. It's an interesting translation of the story into modern language.

In *The Jesus Diaries,* Jesus himself shares his perspective on the events which made him world-famous in an easy-to-read conversational style. Speaking in the first person, Jesus anchors his life in the politically tense, yet exciting days of the first century, as he explains the amazing events that lead up to his birth, and the intrigue that follows him throughout his life.

He gives us insights into the deep meaning of his words and illustrates how his teachings are firmly rooted in the Hebrew Old Testament. He walks us through the moving events of his life as seen through his eyes and introduces us to people in desperate need, whose lives are miraculously changed forever, leaving us breathlessly expectant to see what will happen next.

The Jesus Diaries is based directly on a scholarly, word-by-word analysis and amalgamation of the four Gospels in the New Testament. Like a detective, Helen Hunter exercises her theological training and her background as a translator to meticulously piece together the events of Jesus' life, and to answer so many of the questions left unanswered in the Gospels.

Foreword

A unique feature is Jesus' own account of hundreds of Old Testament prophecies that are linked to his life and teachings. This, together with the rich historical and geographical descriptions, give you the feeling that you are right there in his world, experiencing it all with him.

Helen Hunter's book, *The Jesus Diaries* is an accurate super-amplification of the actual Gospel texts. It is ideally suited to introduce adults and young people to the real Jesus, in language they can understand. Because of its accuracy and rock-solid scriptural foundation, it can be used with confidence in schools, churches and colleges, and to introduce people of all cultural backgrounds to the founder of Christianity.

James R. Adair, Ph. D. in Old and New Testament.

University Professor:
Baptist University of the Americas
B.H. Carroll Theological Institute
Mercer University
Texas Christian University
Southwestern Baptist Theological Seminary
Baptist Theological College, Cape Town

Author of ***Introducing Christianity***
Editor of the Society of Biblical Literature
General Editor of TC: A Journal of Biblical Textual Criticism

Dear Friend,

While I was on earth over two thousand years ago, many people met me, hugged me, talked with me, ate with me and traveled with me.

Now I'm writing to you personally to let you know who I am, where I came from, what I accomplished and where I am today. You may not have met me physically, but I'm hoping that as you read my story, we will become very well acquainted.

Love,
Jesus

MAP OF ISRAEL IN NEW TESTAMENT TIMES

1

Shocking Incident At Work

IT ALL STARTED THE DAY my uncle went to work and came home mute. Try as he might, he just couldn't make a sound. He couldn't tell anyone about the secret message. He couldn't warn them that the incredible predictions everyone had been talking about were about to come true. His voice was completely gone.

That particular morning had begun quite normally. My uncle Zachariah, or Uncle Zach, as we liked to call him, finished his breakfast and got ready for work.

"Bye dear," he said as he picked up his travel bag and kissed my Aunt Beth goodbye. "I'll see you in a few days!"

Uncle Zach came from a long line of priests who worked in the famous temple in Jerusalem over two thousand years ago. The priests all lived in the town of Hebron, about twenty miles away in the hill country, and took turns commuting into the city for work.[1]

Uncle Zach took off briskly down the road past groves of olive and almond trees in the direction of Abraham's grave.

"Lord," he said to God as he walked, *"Abraham must have been really special for you to miraculously give him a son when he was a hundred years old and Sara was ninety! I'm almost as old as Abraham, Lord, and nothing like that has happened for Beth and me.*

"Can miracles still happen to ordinary people like us? You know it would mean the world if we could have just one baby. I

know, I know. We're old enough to be grandparents—even great-grandparents. But Beth says we're young at heart... We're still praying for a miracle, but I'm wondering if we really believe it could happen, or if we are just going through the motions? After all, we are really old. Tell me if we should keep on believing, or are we just deluding ourselves?"

Uncle Zach walked along, deep in thought, over the gentle hills and dry river beds he knew so well. He didn't look up until he reached the outskirts of Jerusalem, the holiest city in the world. When he spotted the dazzling new temple in the distance, he was suddenly filled with wonder. Our people believed that the temple in Jerusalem was the earthly home of God, and every time he saw it, Uncle Zach felt honored to work there.

The temple had been under construction for decades. It rose high into the sky, commanding the respect and awe of everyone who saw it. The temple was part of the ambitious building program of King Herod the Great, and a thousand priests could be found working there on any given day. Uncle Zach couldn't even remember a time when there wasn't some chiseling or hammering going on whenever he arrived for work.

Uncle Zach pushed his personal problem aside and began to think about the day that lay ahead, never dreaming what that day would bring. Coming to work was always exciting and he looked forward to seeing the other priests in his division who worked with him on his shift.[2] Since they were all the direct descendants of Aaron, the very first Hebrew priest, his co-workers were also his tribal brothers and Uncle Zach treated them all as family.

My uncle made his way inside the temple grounds and walked past hundreds of priests who were busy on the

Shocking Incident At Work

construction. That morning they were putting the finishing touches on the glistening white marble columns. Roman guards were monitoring them from the temple roof as usual. As non-Hebrews, they were not allowed to step on the holy ground of the temple itself.

It so happened that Uncle Zach was chosen that morning for a once-in-a-lifetime opportunity to burn the incense inside the temple.

"What a privilege!" he thought, moved by this exciting opportunity. *"Priests have been doing this for almost fifteen hundred years, since the time of Moses and Aaron—and today, I'm the lucky one! Thank you, God. This is a day I've dreamed of my whole career! You knew I needed some encouragement today."*

The priests' job was to do three main things: serve God, bless the people, and keep the incense burning continuously in the temple lamps[3] to remind everyone of the constant presence of God in their lives. Today, Uncle Zach would be the one to refill the lamps with fresh oil and burn sweet-smelling incense on the altar in the morning and again in the evening.[4]

Uncle Zach made his way to the altar, where he carefully started to clean the lamps. In the meantime, a large crowd gathered for the morning service outside, praying and waiting patiently for him to come out and bless them.

As my uncle lit the lamps and breathed the sweet-smelling incense,[5] he thought about how God had led our ancestors across the desert in the form of a pillar of light by night and a cloud by day. God promised to visit them in the form of a cloud inside the temple at the place of forgiveness.[6] *Maybe God would visit him today!*

Uncle Zach was totally engrossed with his task when suddenly, a spirit that looked like an angel appeared on the right side of the altar, at the exact spot where God said his presence would be. Uncle Zach looked up and jumped back, startled. He had read about angels[7] in the holy books and he was terrified, not knowing what would happen next.[8]

2

A Stunning Announcement

"DON'T BE AFRAID, ZACHARIAH," the angel said to my uncle. "I have great news for you. God has heard your prayers and he will give you a son!"

Uncle Zach gasped with emotion as he put his hands to his mouth.

"Your wife, Elizabeth, will give birth to a little baby boy and you will name him John."

"*Beth—pregnant?*" he thought. "*You mean it really could be happening?*"

"You will be thrilled with John," the angel was saying, "and even people outside your family circle will be delighted at his birth. Your son will be great in God's eyes. He will be filled to overflowing with the joyful spirit of God himself, even in his mother's womb, and he will never need to touch a drop of alcohol to be happy."

"*So John would be a Nazarite,*" thought Uncle Zach. These holy men devoted themselves exclusively to serving God and made three special promises. They would not consume anything made from grapes—no wine, strong liquor, vinegar or even raisins; they would not cut their hair; and they would not touch any dead body or animal carcass.[9]

"*How intriguing,*" thought Uncle Zach, flashing back to Samson and Samuel, two other Nazarites born to childless women after they had begged God for a baby. Samson delivered our ancestors from their enemies,[10] and Samuel was a great priest and prophet.[11]

"Your son John," the angel was saying, "will turn the hearts of many true believers back to the Lord their God."

"Then he must be the Messenger!" thought Uncle Zach, stunned. He had read the angel's exact words dozens of times. In the holy books the prophets called the one who would turn the hearts of many the Messenger. *"My boy is the long-awaited Messenger?"*

For centuries, our ancestors had been waiting for a Savior, whom God had kept promising to send them. Before the Savior came, however, the prophet Malachi had predicted that God would send a messenger to prepare the way for him.

"Yes, Zacharaiah," continued the angel, "This son of yours is the Messenger who will blaze a trail for the coming of the expected Savior. He will have the same spirit and power as the prophet, Elijah, who boldly challenged the wicked people of his day to believe in and obey God.

"Your son will confront parents who have given up on their children, and help them love and reach out to them again. He will persuade the most hardened skeptics, who refuse to believe in God, to turn to him. He will start a wave of family reconciliation and prepare people to be ready to receive God with open hearts."

My uncle remembered that this is exactly what Malachi had predicted;[12] but still, he wanted proof.

A Stunning Announcement

"How will I know that this is really going to happen?" he asked the messenger. "I'm old. And Beth? Let's just say that a pregnancy would be physically impossible at this stage!"

"It will happen because I am Gabriel—the messenger of God. My job is to stand in God's presence, ready to carry his messages to people. God himself has personally dispatched me to bring you this birth announcement."

Uncle Zach knew who the angel Gabriel was. He was sent out to reveal secrets to people who prayed a lot,[13] and now Gabriel was talking to him!

"Zachariah, listen to me!" The angel's voice had changed. He was speaking sternly now. "Because you didn't believe me when I said that your wife would get pregnant, here's what's going to happen to you: from this moment forward, you'll not be able to speak until the day when everything I told you about will actually take place."

As you can imagine, Uncle Zach was horrified. He had read the prophet Ezekiel's prediction that God would make a certain man's tongue stick to the roof of his mouth and he would be mute.[14] Never in his wildest dreams did Uncle Zach expect to be like that man! How awful!

But Ezekiel had also predicted that one day that man's mouth would be opened and his voice would return. Then the people would give all the credit to God and everyone would know that the man's muteness had been a sign from God.[15] Uncle Zach was both humbled and awed to find out that he was the one to play that most unwanted role...

While the angel was talking with my uncle, the people out in the courtyard were waiting for him to come out and read the holy books and to pronounce the customary blessing. God himself had instructed Aaron, the first priest, to always give the people the priestly blessing, which went like this: "May the Lord bless you and keep you. May the Lord make his face shine on you and be gracious towards you. May the Lord lift up his face towards you and give you peace."[16]

For fifteen hundred years, right on cue, the priest on duty had repeated these same comforting words before dismissing the worshippers; but today, Uncle Zach was nowhere to be seen and the people wondered why he delayed. What could have happened? Was he alright? They were starting to get anxious.

When Uncle Zach finally emerged, he tried to speak the blessing, but he couldn't. All he could do was wave his arms and use sign language because no sound would come from his lips. The people stared at him, perplexed. He didn't look disoriented, like someone who has just had a stroke. He didn't look spooked, like someone who was in trouble. He looked excited! That's when they realized that he must have seen a vision and they wished he could tell them what had happened.

Uncle Zach finished out his tour of duty in Jerusalem without saying a word. When it was over, he trudged back home to be with Aunt Beth, who of course was surprised that he couldn't talk. It wasn't long after his return, however, that Aunt Beth conceived, just like the angel Gabriel had said she would. For the first five months she hid her pregnancy, enjoying the excitement of it all and dreaming about her future baby. She was so grateful to

A Stunning Announcement

God for giving her a child, because in those days, being childless was considered a terrible curse.¹⁷

"*Thank you, God, for doing this miracle in me,*" Beth prayed. "*Now I don't have to be embarrassed any more. Now I won't feel so different from other women. I too will have a baby like all the rest of them!*"

But before she went public with her good news, there was someone she had to see first...

3

Unusual Answer To Prayer

WHILE ALL THIS WAS GOING on in Hebron at Uncle Zach's house, other exciting events were taking place up in the northern part of the country—and that's where I come in. My story begins at about the time when my Aunt Beth was in her sixth month of pregnancy. That is when God dispatched the angel Gabriel on another mission.

Gabriel was typically sent to people who prayed a lot.[18] This time, his destination was Nazareth, a village in Galilee. He was dispatched to a young woman who was to become my mother. Her name was Maryam, or Mary in English. She was a single young girl, still living a very sheltered life at home. My grandparents had set up an arranged marriage for her. She was engaged to be married one day to a very respectable man named Joseph, a direct descendant of the great King David, but until that time came, she continued to live with her parents.

Mary stayed close to home and learned to do household chores, while her older brothers left for work every day. Her village was just outside Sepphoris, the regional capital. Sepphoris was a bustling, cosmopolitan center on the main trade route from the Mediterranean Sea to the Far East. A fortified walled city set on a hill, it enjoyed spectacular views of shimmering Lake Galilee in the distance. But the people in the village of

Nazareth lived a more modest life, growing crops to sell in the marketplaces in the city, and commuting in for construction jobs and day labor.

When the angel Gabriel appeared to Mary, he complimented her.

"Hello, Mary," he said. "I've come to tell you that God is very pleased with you. He's been watching over you for years, and he has selected you from all the other women on earth for a very special task."

When my mother heard the angel's words, she was pleasantly surprised and very intrigued.

"*I wonder what he means?*" she thought. "What kind of a task has God chosen me for?"

"Don't be afraid, Mary," said the angel. "You have wanted God's approval for a long time. He has heard your prayers and he will use you. I have come to let you know that you are the virgin who will soon become pregnant and give birth to the long awaited Savior!"

"That's it! The special sign!" my mother remembered excitedly. As a devout Hebrew girl, she knew all about the special sign. The prophet Isaiah had predicted that God would give our people a special sign, so they would be able to recognize the Savior when he came. It was the sign of the virgin! "A virgin will miraculously become pregnant and give birth to a son. She will call the baby Immanuel, which means 'God is with us'.[19] He will be a wonderful boy and one day, he'll govern the whole world!" the prophet had written.

All these words were flashing through my mother's mind as the heavenly messenger continued.

"You are that virgin, and you will name your baby Yeshua, or Savior," which in English is Joshua or Jesus. "He is the son of the most high God, and he will be great. In fact, God will give him the throne of his ancestor, King David, and he'll rule over the Hebrew people forever."

"This is incredible!" my mother thought. "I'm part of God's epic plan. But wait... How can I have a baby if I'm a virgin? I know that an angel promised our ancestor, Sara, a child in her old age, but she had Abraham."

"How is this actually going to happen," Mary asked the angel, "seeing that I've never had an intimate relationship with a man?"

The heavenly messenger's explanation was amazing:

"The holy breath of God himself will come over you and the power of God will completely cover you. This power will be so great that it will create a new life in you. The child born from your body will be totally holy, set apart for a special purpose, because he will be called the Son of God."

"This is awesome," thought my mother.

"As a matter of fact," the angel was saying, "your cousin Elizabeth, who hasn't been able to get pregnant in all these years, has also received a wonderful surprise. She's in the sixth month of her pregnancy even as we speak. That's because with God nothing is impossible and every word he says will come to pass."

"Beth pregnant?" thought my mother. "My cousin is a wrinkled old lady! But then Abraham's wife, Sara, was older than most grandmothers when she got pregnant! That just proves that there is nothing too hard for God. He creates amazing miracles and causes wonderful things to happen, that are way beyond human powers or even their expectations."

"When Beth's pregnancy comes full term," the angel told my mother, "she, too, will have a baby boy!"

My mother believed everything the angel told her. "If Aunt Beth is pregnant, and God says he'll create a baby in me without the help of a man, I know he will do it!" she told herself. Her response to Gabriel was clear:

"I am God's willing servant," she replied. "Tell God that I'm ready to obey his powerful command. I surrender myself completely to him. I'm ready for him to carry out his orders in my body and in my life."

Having successfully delivered his message, the angel Gabriel said goodbye to my mother and left Nazareth to return to heaven and stand by God's side. His mission was accomplished. Meanwhile, my mother's mind was already racing ahead...

4

Surprise Family Reunion

AS SOON AS ANGEL GABRIEL left, my mother couldn't wait to check out how Aunt Beth's pregnancy was going and share her own wonderful news. Women didn't ever travel alone in those days, but some of her relatives were headed to Jerusalem, so she grabbed a few belongings and walked south with them as far as Uncle Zach's house in Hebron.

"Hello! Beth? Are you home?" she called out when she walked in the door. "It's me, your cousin Mary!"

As soon as Aunt Beth heard my mother's voice in the distance, she felt the baby inside her jump for joy. The holy breath of God filled her heart and she rushed excitedly to greet my mother.

"Mary! Look at you! You're the luckiest woman on earth! And the baby you're carrying is the greatest gift the world has ever seen! So why are you, the mother of my Lord, coming to visit me?"

How did Aunt Beth know all this? The two women hadn't shared secrets yet, but God had already revealed everything to Aunt Beth and she was ecstatic.

"The instant I heard your voice calling out to me," she said, "I felt my baby jump for joy inside my belly! I think he recognized the holy one that you are carrying! I'm feeling really wonderful, and I know that God will be good to you too. Do you know why?"

My mother looked at her, intrigued.

"Why?" she asked.

"Because you believed the message!"

"I did!" said Mary. "I'm so excited I feel like I'm going to burst! I'm really thankful to God for his goodness. Do you realize that he has chosen me to have his baby, even though I've done nothing to deserve it? I keep asking myself: *'Why me? I'm just a young girl from a humble family!'* I always thought that only the rich and famous, the talented and the wealthy got God's attention. I realize now that God often picks unknown people just like me."

"That's what I used to think too," said Aunt Beth, "especially as I got older and everyone else was having a baby except for me! But look at me now!"

"I know how you feel!" said my mother. "You know, I always thought that our long-awaited Savior would be famous and powerful like the people in the big city; but God has decided to give him to a totally unknown girl like me! Do you realize that from now on, all future generations are going to consider me really special and really fortunate because of this?"

Aunt Beth smiled at her with an understanding look.

"I've been thinking how amazing this all is!" my mother was chattering happily. "God lives up in heaven where there is nothing but beauty and joy—but he cares enough to be interested in us down here! He humbles himself to look at things that are happening on earth. He spots proud, arrogant people who think of themselves as better than everyone else and topples tyrants from their thrones. At the same time, he feels the experiences of ordinary people like us as if he were right here,[20] and he lifts completely unknown people into important positions of prominence that they never would have reached on their own!"

"You know, Mary," said Aunt Beth, "since I've been pregnant, I've had a lot of time to think about the great heroes of the faith like Noah, who built the ark and escaped from the flood; Abraham, who loved God enough to obey him when God asked him to offer him his son; and Moses, who led our ancestors out of slavery in Egypt; like David, who killed the giant Goliath; and Job, who lost all his children and all his possessions, yet never cursed God. What I've realized is that they all recognized God's greatness and admired him from the depths of their hearts."

"And we do too, don't we, Beth?" said my mother.

"You know, it's so great to have you here to talk to, Mary," said her cousin. "Stay with us a while. We have plenty of room, and you can help me get ready for the baby!"

My mother was thrilled to be with Aunt Beth and to hear everything that God was doing in her life, so she decided to stay until John was born. They were able to spend a lot of time together, since Uncle Zach was mute at that time and couldn't talk, and Aunt Beth was glad for the company.

5

The Miracle Baby

AUNT BETH'S DUE DATE GREW closer and closer, until she finally went into labor and delivered a healthy baby boy.

"Oh, look, Zach!" she cried for joy. "Look at our beautiful baby boy! He has ten fingers and ten toes, just like every other healthy baby! Isn't he just perfect? Oh, God! Thank you, thank you, thank you! We have our very own son! How can we ever thank you enough for this miracle?"

Uncle Zach was overjoyed too, but he was still speechless. When the neighbors and relatives heard the good news, they were thrilled. They all made plans to go to Hebron for the baby's circumcision ceremony.[21]

Most of the tribes around us used circumcision as a rite of passage to manhood around the age of thirteen. However, God had specifically ordered our ancestor Abraham to circumcise every Hebrew male as a newborn. The order applied to every baby boy, whether born directly into a Hebrew home, or whether purchased for adoption or slavery from a close relative, or even from an enemy.[22]

The ceremony was to take place on the eighth day, as a mark of God's ownership of the child from birth. It was also the time designated to name the baby. Of course, the family members automatically called the baby Zachariah Junior, after my Uncle Zach. But Aunt Beth put her foot down.

"No! The baby's name will be John!" she declared.

"But you don't have any relatives on either side of the family called John!" they protested. They looked at Uncle Zach and asked what he wanted to call the baby. Uncle Zach signaled them to bring a tablet for him to write on.

"His name is John," he wrote, and he held the tablet up for all to see. They were all surprised by this unusual departure from tradition. However, as soon as Uncle Zach finished writing the words, his voice suddenly returned and he burst out laughing with joy and praising God.

"Look! I can talk! Oh, thank you God!" he exclaimed loudly. "This is awesome!" Tears of gratitude were pouring down Uncle Zach's face as he hugged Beth and everyone around him and went to pick up the baby for all to see.

"Quick, everyone! Gather around! Now that I have my voice back, I can finally tell you all about the secret message!"

Of course, they all gathered around to hear what he had to say after almost a year of silence. They had all been wondering what was going on. The suspense was unbearable! Uncle Zach cleared his throat. All eyes were focused intently on him; everyone leaned forward expectantly, eager to find out what the secret message was all about.

"I have an important announcement!" Uncle Zach declared. "Our God is awesome, and amazing things are about to happen! I have proof now that the Savior we have been expecting for centuries will be here very soon! He will pay the ransom for all our sins—so we can be free!"

Everyone gasped. *"What's going on?"* they wondered.

The Miracle Baby

"I've had a lot of time to think during these long months of silence, and now I want to let it all out. You remember the day I lost my voice?"

They all nodded. How could they forget? That's when he had come back from the temple and couldn't talk. They all wondered if he had seen a vision.

"I did see a vision when I was back there cleaning the lamps," he told them. "The angel Gabriel himself came to me and told me that our baby, little John here, is the long-awaited Messenger who is supposed to announce that the Savior is already on his way!"

Everyone started talking at once. "Baby John is the Messenger? So the Savior really is coming soon? How soon?" they all wanted to know.

"I've been thinking about the current political situation," Uncle Zach replied. "This Roman occupation feels just like the slavery our ancestors suffered when they were in Egypt and God sent Moses to set them free.[23] Well, now God's Savior is on his way to deliver us—and I'm overcome with joy about it!

"I know you've been expecting the Savior all your lives. Remember how God gave Abraham and Sara a son in their old age, and promised to bless the nations of the world through him? But then the unthinkable happened! God tested Abraham by asking him to sacrifice his miracle boy and with him, give up all his dreams. Abraham didn't hesitate. He started up the mountain, trusting God for a miracle.

"Fortunately for all of us, God stopped Abraham just in time! He rewarded his obedience by promising to make his descendants as numerous as the stars of heaven, or the grains of sand on the seashore.[24] In addition, he promised to bless all the nations of the earth through one specific descendant of Abraham's[25]—the Savior we have been expecting for centuries. And now, dear friends, we are the lucky ones who will get to see the Savior with our very own eyes!"[26]

Uncle Zach's words were electrifying! The people listened as he continued to reveal the meaning of everything that was happening:

"You know that through the ages, the prophets who wrote and spoke on God's behalf kept this promise alive. Over and over again they repeated God's unconditional guarantee to Abraham that one of his descendants, through King David's line, would be the Savior of the world.

"God already has this Savior standing in the wings!" said Uncle Zach excitedly. "He will snatch us from the dominating power of our enemies, so that we'll be free to serve God without fear!

"And you, my little baby John," he said, looking down into his newborn's sleepy little eyes, "you will be called a prophet, a spokesman of the most high God! You are the Messenger[27] who will prepare the paths in which he will walk. You are the one that the prophet Isaiah wrote about when he spoke of a voice crying out, saying: 'Prepare the way of the Lord in the wilderness and make a straight highway in the desert for our God!'[28] Just like when a king travels to a far country and the roads are repaired and made level and smooth for him, you will make it easy for our Savior King to come to us!

"You, my son, will explain to our people that the gift of forgiveness is coming to us. You will announce to them that we can be forgiven for all of our wrongdoing and released from all guilt and condemnation! God wants to show us his love and mercy; he doesn't want to punish us like we deserve. He is good to all people; his tenderness, understanding and sensitivity are clearly seen in everything he does."[29]

Uncle Zach's friends and relatives nodded their heads in agreement.

"Because of God's love," Uncle Zach was saying, "a brilliant ray of sunshine from heaven has shined on us and examined us closely. This ray of sunshine will take care of us by coming to earth and giving us light!"

Uncle Zach was so inspired that he couldn't stop talking; and the people in the room were mesmerized, hanging on his every word.

"The prophet Zechariah predicted that in a single day the Savior will remove the guilty verdict from us.[30] He will be a king and a priest, and he will give us advice that will bring peace to the world.[31] He will not judge us by our outward appearance, looking only at what he sees. He will not condemn us based only on what he hears. He will look at what is in our hearts.[32]

"The prophet Malachi predicted that he will heal all our sicknesses if we look to God and obey him.[33] The prophet Isaiah predicted that he will come to light up an escape route for us when we are stuck in spiritual darkness, facing the perils of life alone and without divine guidance.[34]

"The Savior is coming to open the eyes of the blind among us, and to bring those of us who are miserable out from our personal hell.[35] He will call those of us who can't stop sinning and making ourselves wrong and feeling guilty all the time, to come out into his light and finally be set free to enjoy life in all its fullness!"[36]

"Listen to me, friends and family! The Savior is coming soon! With the birth of little John here, it's only a matter of a few years now…"

Everyone was profoundly touched by Uncle Zach's words. They marveled that Aunt Beth had been able to bear a child in her old age, and that Uncle Zach's voice had come back. Above all, they couldn't wait to rush out and tell everyone the great news that the Savior was actually on his way!

Within days, word had spread like wildfire throughout the hill country, from Hebron all the way to Jerusalem. Uncle Zach's excitement about the coming Savior was contagious, and all the people who lived in the area were filled with awe and reverence for God.

"What kind of a man is this miracle baby destined to be?" they all wondered.

They had no idea that my little cousin would grow up to become an amazing man, who would be physically and spiritually strong. They didn't know then that he would be a man of prayer. They didn't foresee that he would spend his youth in remote, desolate areas of the country alone with God, like so many of God's prophets before him, until the day when he would go public and be presented to the nation.

6

Embarrassing Situation Resolved

A FEW MONTHS AFTER MY mother returned back to Nazareth, it eventually became obvious that she was pregnant. Her fiancé, Joseph, knew that the baby wasn't his, since he hadn't been intimate with her. Naturally, he assumed that she had been with another man.

"No, I haven't," Mary insisted. "God is the one who made me pregnant!"

"Yeah, right!" thought Joseph. He didn't believe her for a second. Being older than she was, he couldn't be fooled. Based on God's law, if a man found something disgraceful in his wife's or his fiancée's conduct, he could write her a letter of divorce, hand it to her, and send her on her way.[37] Legally, he had no obligation to marry her.

But Joseph was a kind man. He realized that an unmarried pregnant teenager could be judged by the religious leaders and stoned to death immediately. The holy books said that if an engaged or married woman slept with another man, both she and the man were to be put to death.[38] Joseph loved God and wanted to be kind like God; he also loved Mary too much to make a public spectacle of her and force her go through such a cruel and painful death.

At first he thought he would be discreet and privately release her from the engagement; but as he was strategizing about his predicament, he had a dream. In the dream, a glowing angel of the Lord appeared to him.

"Joseph, descendant of the great King David, don't be afraid to marry Mary," the angel said. "Go ahead and have the wedding ceremony! The baby she is carrying is not a man's baby. Mary is telling the truth. The breath of God himself conceived this baby. This child is the long-awaited Holy One who is supposed to be born to a virgin."

Joseph was humbled and relieved to hear the truth about the pregnancy.

"Mary will give birth to a son," the angel told him. "And you will give him a name that describes his character. That name is Jesus, which means Savior, because he will save the people from their sins. He will deliver them from their inability to be in relationship with God. He will save them from the punishment they rightly deserve, because they have knowingly disobeyed his laws.

"Everything that has happened here is part of God's plan, as predicted by the prophet Isaiah. A virgin will conceive and give birth to a son."[39]

When Joseph awoke from his dream, he was awed at his new role in God's plan. He was familiar with the prophet Isaiah's prediction about the virgin who would conceive, so he decided to love and accept me and raise me as his own. He got up and did exactly what the heavenly messenger had ordered him to do. He took my mother back into his life and heart and they had the wedding. However, they didn't become intimate until after I was born.

7

Teenager Gives Birth In Motel Shed

THE AREA WHERE MY PARENTS lived was controlled by the Roman Empire. The empire extended from today's Spain as far as Syria, and from Germany to Africa, and throughout most of the known world. The Roman Emperor at that time was Augustus Caesar, the adopted son of Julius Caesar. He liked to call himself Son of God, because he wanted people to know how important he was.

Every few years, the Romans would take a population census or do a property tax review. Shortly before I was due to be born, Augustus Caesar ordered all people under Roman control to return to their home town and register in the population census there. The census was a huge inconvenience, but people had no choice. They had to obey the emperor's orders, or brutal consequences would follow.

That particular census was supervised by the Governor of Syria, the Roman Senator Quirinius, otherwise known as Cyrenius, who was a high level military commander in the Roman army.

Since my stepfather was directly descended from King David, whose hometown was Bethlehem, that's where he had to go to register for the census. He had to take my mother with him on this mandatory trip, as she was now legally his wife. He let her ride the family donkey to make the journey more comfortable for her, because by this time she was very pregnant. The two of them left the low-lying plains of Nazareth and traveled up to the mountainous area of David's home town of Bethlehem.

Walking from town to town was dangerous because there was a lot of looting going on. People resented being so heavily taxed by the occupying forces so there was a lot of civil unrest and desperate people were out on the open road. It was a long walk, lasting several days, slowed down by my mother's pregnancy.

Bethlehem was about five miles outside Jerusalem, on the main road that comes up from Egypt. It was an ideal stopping point for pilgrims and merchants going on to the capital. Back then, there were no private rooms for rent along the way. Travelers would stay at roadside motels that were like one big dormitory.

As soon as they reached Bethlehem, my mother's contractions began and she went into labor. Because there was no privacy in the communal dorm, my stepfather took her to a cattle shed next door and called for a local midwife to help them with the delivery.

After I was born, my mother took some strips of cloth she had brought with her and wrapped me into a tight little bundle, as they used to do with babies back then. She laid me down in a crib, which normally served as a feeding trough for the animals that slept inside the shed during the winter.

Then my stepfather broke with tradition, just like Uncle Zach had. He didn't name me Joseph Junior. Instead, he named me Yeshua, or Jesus in English—which means Deliverer.

8

The Party In The Sky

THAT SAME NIGHT, SOME LOCAL shepherds were watching their flocks out in the open fields near Bethlehem. It wasn't too cold yet to sleep outdoors, so they worked in shifts; some slept while others were on guard duty, watching for wild animals.

During the night watch, the same angel that had spoken to my stepfather, Joseph, suddenly appeared to the shepherds. He was surrounded by a brilliant light and glowed brightly because he had come from the presence of God. The shepherds on duty were absolutely terrified and wanted to run away. Their screams of panic woke the others, but the angel spoke to them.

"Don't be afraid!" the angel said. "I've brought you some fantastic news!" The light of God's presence lit up the whole night sky around him and the shepherds stopped to listen.

"I've come to tell you that today the long awaited Savior, chosen and sent by God to save the world, has finally been born right here in Bethlehem!" the angel announced. "This news is so exciting that millions of people all around the world will jump for joy when they hear it."

Even the shepherds had heard about the promise that a special child would be born to a virgin and one day rule the world.[40] They listened in amazement as the angel continued:

"This is how you will know that what I'm saying is true. Go back into town and you'll find a little baby lying in a manger and wrapped in cloth. When you see the little bundle of joy—he's the one!"

Suddenly, the shepherds saw vast numbers of angelic beings appear and join the angel in praising God. The shepherds had heard about angels, but they had never seen one! Now they watched in amazement as hundreds of them came into view.

"Wow!" said one of the shepherds. "This is just like when Abraham's grandson, Jacob, saw a host of angels climbing up and down a ladder to heaven!"[41]

"Yeah!" said another. "Now I know what it felt like!"[42]

"And the angels look even more brilliant and shiny than Moses!" said one of the eldest in the group. "They say that he virtually glowed when he came down from Mt. Sinai when God gave him the Law and the Ten Commandments, and these beings are lighting up the whole sky!"[43]

"King David said that angels are really strong beings," said another old shepherd.

"They are constantly listening for the voice of God, ready to hear his word and obey his orders!" said another.[44]

"The prophet Daniel had a vision of heaven," said a young shepherd. "He saw a million angels waiting on God, and a billion angels standing before him. Could we be seeing into heaven right now?"[45]

As the shepherds listened, they heard the angels say:

"Congratulations, Lord God in the highest heaven, on the birth of your first-born son! We wish blessings and peace to all good people who love you."

The Party In The Sky

Eventually, the angels took off and went back up to heaven. As soon as the last one disappeared from view, the shepherds burst out talking amongst themselves.

"This is incredible!" they exclaimed.

"Let's go to Bethlehem and check it out and see the baby for ourselves!" said one of the younger ones.

"Yes, let's just go right now!" said their leader. So they hurried into town and found my mother and my stepfather in the cattle shed next to the motel, just as the angel had described.

"Can we take a peek at the baby?" they asked.

"Sure!" said my stepfather proudly. "Come on in!"

"The angels were right! They told us we would find him here!"

The shepherds were thrilled to see me with their own eyes. They could hardly wait to rush over to the motel dormitory next door to spread the news. Then they ran from house to house, waking everyone to let them know what the angels had said about me. They told everyone that the long awaited Savior was already here on earth, in the shed next to the inn! Those who heard were amazed at the news.

The shepherds went back to their homes, whistling and singing and thanking God for all the wonderful things they had seen and heard. As they walked, they talked in amazement about what the angel had said.

Meanwhile, my mother kept all these precious moments in her heart and thought about them from time to time. She remembered our ancestor Jacob. His son, also named Joseph, was a visionary. Jacob had seen angels and was very open to the spiritual dimension of his son. He paid very careful attention to the growing boy and quietly protected him from his cruel, but more practical brothers.[46]

My mother realized that amazing things had happened around my birth. She planned to watch me very carefully, just like Jacob had watched his son Joseph, and see how my life unfolded.

9

Elderly Couple Predicts Future

AFTER MY BIRTH, MY MOTHER was considered ritually unclean for forty days and had to go through the purification process prescribed in the holy books. Fortunately for her, I was a boy, because for the mothers of girl babies, the process took exactly twice as long.[47]

During that first week, she went through a series of cleansing procedures to be ready for the traditional eighth day—the day of my circumcision ceremony. This was a day of great celebration. According to the holy books, every first-born of man and beast belonged to God,[48] and had to be bought back from him by the eighth day.[49]

At the ceremony, I was officially named Jesus, or Joshua, which means Savior—the name given to me by the angel before I was ever conceived. As the first-born son, I was given special rights as the head of the family, and I was entitled to double honor and a double inheritance.[50]

For thirty-two more days, my mother was not allowed to enter the temple or touch any sacred object and she had to continue to purify herself. After that, she had to take a sacrifice to the priest in Jerusalem, at which time she would be considered clean.[51]

The sacrifice was to be a lamb less than one year old. It would be roasted in the fire to buy back my life from God. In addition, she was to bring a bird to pay for any wrongdoing she might have committed. It could be a pigeon or a turtle-dove. If she couldn't afford the lamb, she could bring two young pigeons or two doves to the temple door instead.

When my mother's forty days were up, my parents took the required sacrifices and carried me up to the temple in Jerusalem, just five miles up the road from Bethlehem, to present me to God.

At that time, there was a man named Simeon living in Jerusalem. He was a very spiritual man, who desperately wanted to please God. Years back, God had revealed to Simeon that he would not die until he had seen the long-expected Savior with his own eyes. Simeon was familiar with the prophet Isaiah's promise of comfort, and he was constantly on the lookout for this Savior.[52] While he waited with great expectation, he lived a life of obedient service, careful not to offend either God or man.

On the very day that my parents brought me into the temple for the customary presentation ceremony, God's holy Spirit led Simeon to get up and go to the temple, to the exact spot where we were standing. As soon as he saw me, Simeon instantly knew in his heart who I was. He rushed over to us and reached out eagerly to pick me up in his arms. My mother instinctively let him. Simeon carefully picked me up and gently cradled me in his arms. Visibly moved, he studied my tiny little face.

"Dear God!" he said with profound gratitude, "Now you can release me, your humble servant, to die in peace. And please let the rest of humanity see him also, so they too can die in peace." Tears of joy were streaming down his face. Then Simeon held me up high and spun me around in a little dance of joy.

"This baby is the hope and glorious light of the Hebrew people," he declared. "The prophet Isaiah predicted a great future, when God's light would come into the world and people everywhere would come to that light. Even kings will come from far and near to see the brightness of his spectacular rise!"[53]

"What's even more amazing," continued Simeon, holding me gently against his chest, "is that this baby will reveal God's secrets to all people everywhere, Hebrew or not! Isaiah predicted that the people who walked in darkness and ignorance will see a great light.[54]

"We've glimpsed the light of God in the words of the priestly blessing which says: 'May the Lord make his face shine upon you.'[55] We've glimpsed the light of God when he led our ancestors through the wilderness to the Promised Land in a pillar of fire. We've glimpsed the light of God in the lamp burning continuously in the temple.

"But now the real light is here! This is wonderful! The prophet Isaiah predicted that when the Savior comes, all the ends of the earth will benefit.[56] He said that this baby will be a light to all peoples, regardless of race, color or creed, because he will bring God's salvation to the ends of the earth."[57]

My parents were amazed that Simeon recognized who I was. Simeon blessed them both and then he stepped in close to speak directly to my mother.

"Mary," he said, "this son of yours is destined to either lift up—or trip up—many of our people. The prophet Isaiah predicted that he will be a refuge and a place of safety for many; but he will also be a stumbling block to the houses of Israel and a snare that can trap the inhabitants of Jerusalem.[58]

"The prophet Hosea predicted that ordinary people, who are honest with others and obedient to God, will enjoy walking with God. But those who are headstrong and independent of God will be easily seduced and led astray. They will fall flat on their faces because of this Savior, and suffer the horrible consequences of sin in their lives."[59]

"Your baby will grow up to become a leader of a radical group of Hebrews who will be severely criticized and persecuted. You yourself, Mary, will go through the most terrible pain and suffering, as though a sword pierced through your very heart. Your heart will be crushed so that the negative thoughts, doubts and quarrels of many other hearts may be supernaturally revealed and brought out into the light."

My mother and stepfather were shocked to hear such a terrible prediction. *"What is Simeon saying, and what does it mean?"* they both wondered as he gave me back to my mother. We watched Simeon turn and leave, his arms high in the air in praise and gratitude to God.

It was almost time to go, but there was one other person in the temple we still had to meet. Besides Simeon, there was an eighty-four-year-old widow there who also recognized me. She was a prophetess who relayed messages from God to the people. Her name was Anna, and she was from the tribe of Asher.

Anna had been married for only seven years when her husband died and she had never re-married. Instead, she devoted herself to worshipping God day and night with prayer, voluntary fasting, and sharing God's words with the people who came to worship. She was always in the temple compound. That is how she came to be standing close by, at the exact time and place that my parents were there to officially present me to God. When she spotted me, she recognized immediately who I was and came right over to meet me.

"Can I hold him?" she asked, reaching out to rock me in her arms.

"This is amazing!" she told my parents. "I'm so thankful to God that I was here to meet the baby! I'm so excited! I'm going to tell everyone who comes into the temple how I personally met the Savior and that he is the one who will pay the ransom for everyone's sins and set us all free!"

10

Astrologers Spot Famous Star

I WAS STILL AN INFANT in Bethlehem when some stargazers arrived in Jerusalem from east of the Jordan River, looking for me. They knew of the ancient Hebrew prophecies about the coming Savior King. They knew that this king would be a descendant of Abraham's grandson Jacob. They also knew he would one day rule from Jerusalem.

Back home, these learned astrologers had searched the skies every night for clues pointing to this king's arrival.[60] They believed that once he was born, his star would shine so brightly in the heavens that everyone—from lowly pagans—to kings and emperors—would see its light. One night they had spotted an exceptionally bright star they had never seen before. They knew exactly what that meant. They had been planning for this moment for years and their bags were packed.

Filled with excitement, they immediately saddled their one-humped dromedary camels, which were bred and trained for speed, and set off to follow the star that would lead them to the king. They took extra camels with them to carry provisions for the trip, as well as the special royal gifts, which they had been saving just for this occasion. After many days' journey, they arrived in Jerusalem and eagerly started asking people questions.

Astrologers Spot Famous Star

"We're looking for the king of the Hebrews who was born here recently," they told everyone. "We saw his star in the east. It's the star of Jacob, signaling the birth of one of his descendants who is coming to rule and reign from Jerusalem. Have you seen him? Do you know where he is?"

Well, the only Hebrew king at that time was King Herod the Great. Herod was not descended from Jacob, but from his rival—his twin-brother, Esau! Centuries earlier, Esau had been born just minutes before Jacob, so he was entitled to inherit his father's wealth and blessing. But Jacob, his younger twin, tricked Esau into selling him his birthright for a bowl of meat and vegetable soup. As a result, Esau lost his inheritance and the twin brothers turned into lifelong enemies.

Jacob's descendants had settled in the area between Galilee and Jerusalem and looked for the Savior to come from their side of the family. Esau's descendants, on the other hand, had settled in Idumaea, the Greek name for Edom, south of Jerusalem. They became known as the Edomites, and they periodically fought to get control of Jerusalem for themselves. The conflict between the two sides of the family had gone on like this for centuries, as each side wanted control of the holy city.

By the time I was born, King Herod the Edomite had been ruling in Jerusalem for about forty years. When he first took over as king after his father was assassinated, our people became furious that yet again, an Edomite was to rule over them. How could the royal Savior King ever come if Jacob's descendants were not in power?

But Herod worked hard to please the conquered Hebrews by rebuilding the temple in Jerusalem, where Uncle Zach worked.

He worked hard to please his Roman bosses by building a massive fortress and a great port on the Mediterranean Sea, which earned him the title of Herod the Great. In addition, he fought off enemy attacks and saved the city of Jerusalem from destruction. After that there was no doubt that he was the uncontested ruler of the region and nobody dared oppose him.

Over the years, however, King Herod had become more and more paranoid. He suffered from high blood pressure and depression. He often threw fits and went into violent rages. He was suspicious of everyone, constantly watching his back and worrying about who might betray him. So when he heard that there was a delegation of learned astrologers looking for a king descended from Jacob's side, and not from Esau's—he was alarmed.

So too, were the people of Jerusalem, because they didn't want yet another war between the two rival families. The news was spreading fast and everyone was wondering what was going on and who the real king should be!

Politically smart, King Herod decided to solve the problem quickly before it got out of hand, so he called an emergency meeting of the Hebrew religious leaders. He specifically requested the presence of the religious professors and scholars called scribes. They were the ones who knew all the details of the ancient texts. They were the experts in all the commandments that God had given to our ancestors through Moses on Mt. Sinai, and they kept up with all the religious traditions that had developed through the ages.

Their job was to teach even the most uneducated people how to apply the commandments in God's holy books to their daily lives. As such, they were highly respected as teachers and professors and the people called them rabbis or master teachers. Because of their intimate knowledge of religious law, these scholars also acted as unpaid judges in religious disputes. They would for sure be able to tell him whether this threat was real.

Herod also assembled the heads of the twenty-four main priestly families, who were called the chief priests, because he wanted to know what they knew.

"I demand to be told where this supposed king of the Hebrews is predicted to be born!" he said.

"Right here in Judea," they all called out at once; "just down the street—in the little village of Bethlehem."

"How can you be so sure?" asked Herod.

"Because the prophet Micah wrote that Bethlehem, the birthplace of King David, would also be the birthplace of a great Hebrew ruler," they said. "His coming has been predicted through the ages and he's been expected since ancient times."[61]

Relieved that he had so quickly and easily solved the riddle, King Herod dismissed the assembly and secretly called the astrologers in for a private meeting.

"Exactly how long has it been since the eastern star first appeared to you, gentlemen?" King Herod asked them sweetly.

"It's been a couple of years," they replied.

"Well then, it's been way too long!" he said, pretending to be sincere. "I insist that you leave immediately to look for this baby king. Go to Bethlehem at once and knock on every door. Ask everyone you see if they know where he is. Leave no stone unturned, and when you find him, come back right away and report directly to me. I want to be the first to know where he is, so I may go down there myself and worship him!"

The astrologers listened to everything the king said, thanked him, and left immediately for Bethlehem. When they looked up at the night sky, they were amazed that the star, which they had followed from the east, started to move forward again. As they rode along, the most learned of the wise men shared what he knew about Bethlehem.

"Centuries ago," he said, "Abraham's grandson, Jacob, settled in Bethlehem. Rachel, his second wife, was the love of his life, but for years she couldn't get pregnant and wept bitter tears. 'Give me children,' she kept begging Jacob, 'or I'll die!'[62]

"After years of embarrassment and anguish, she finally had a baby called Joseph; but his half-brothers were jealous of Joseph and sold him into slavery. Fortunately for Joseph, God had other plans and eventually he rose to the position of right-hand-man to the Pharaoh of Egypt and saved his family from famine.

"Later in life, Rachel had a second child: little Benjamin. However, there were complications during labor and tragically, Rachel died in childbirth. Her husband, beside himself with grief, buried her in Bethlehem.[63] Over the centuries, Benjamin's children and grandchildren multiplied. Now, many of the inhabitants of Bethlehem are Rachel's direct descendants," the wise man explained.

The other astrologers were so intrigued by the story of Rachel that they almost didn't notice that the star had stopped directly over our home in Bethlehem. When they realized that it wasn't moving anymore, they took it as a sign and knocked on our door. I was about two years old when they arrived. The astrologers were overcome with awe and immediately fell to their knees and adored me.

Astrologers Spot Famous Star

Out of their travel bags they pulled treasures they had brought along as gifts. They presented me with gold, the most precious of metals and usually reserved for royalty. They also gave me frankincense, a very expensive incense, which comes from a tree that only grows in Oman and Somalia and is used to consecrate the religious priesthood. Last but not least, they gave me myrrh, a dark, sticky ointment brought from Arabia by the Nabateans of Petra, and used as medicine.

The holy books had predicted that kings from very far away would bring me gifts.[64] Multitudes of one-humped camels would come from the Gulf of Aqaba and the Red Sea; they would bring precious gifts and be filled with praise for the Lord.[65] My mother tells me that I was fascinated by the sparkling treasures and reached out to touch them all eagerly. Little did I know that they symbolized that I was destined to be a king, a priest and a healer.

11

Death Threats Force Family To Flee

THE ASTROLOGERS DECIDED TO spend the night in Bethlehem with their camels. But while they were sleeping, one of them had a dream. In the dream, God warned them not to return to see King Herod. He immediately woke the others up and they held an emergency meeting.

"Let's take a different route and not tell Herod a thing!" they agreed, and left Bethlehem under cover of darkness.

Amazingly, my stepfather also had a dream that night. In the dream, the angel of the Lord appeared to him, surrounded by a gleaming light.

"Get up, Joseph!" the angel insisted. "Take the boy and his mother and escape to Egypt at once. King Herod is sending search parties to Bethlehem to look for the child and kill him. Stay in Egypt until I tell you it's safe to come back."

My stepfather got up right away and shook my mother awake.

"Quick," he said, "We've got to get out of here. Our lives are in danger!" They grabbed me and we left for Egypt in the middle of the night.

When King Herod the Great realized that the astrologers had tricked him, he was furious and flew into a rage. Palace insiders were whispering that he was becoming increasingly suspicious and violent. Many feared he was going crazy.

Death Threats Force Family To Flee

Herod called immediately for his special forces and dispatched them on a top-priority mission.

"I want you to find all the male children in Bethlehem and the surrounding areas and kill them on the spot!" he ordered. "Storm into every house and slaughter every little boy two years old and younger," he said, because, according to the astrologers, that's how far back the star had appeared. "Be thorough!" he threatened, because he didn't want me slipping through his fingers and surviving the extermination campaign.

The special forces took off and did exactly what King Herod the Great commanded them. They forced their way into every home, looking for little baby boys. They tore infants from their screaming mothers' arms and examined them. If they were girls, they tossed them back at their mothers in disgust; but if they were boys, they killed them right in front of their families and then rushed out to catch the next house by surprise.

It wasn't long before the whole town was wailing in shock and disbelief. How could this have happened to their innocent little babies? Why would the soldiers do such a thing? And why did they just pick on the boys? Parents were sobbing and hugging each other, stunned. It made no sense! Others ran around checking to see if the other children were alright, and to comfort the little baby girls that were crying.

Then, what the prophet Jeremiah had predicted centuries earlier happened. A voice was heard crying in Rama, close to Bethlehem, in the area of the tribe of Rachel's son, Benjamin. It was a voice of great mourning and bitter weeping. It was as if Rachel, their ancestral great-great-grandmother, was crying for all her little children—and she would not be comforted, because they were dead and lifeless..."[66]

Once again, the feud between Jacob's clan and Esau's clan was alive and well. Once again a descendant of Esau – King Herod the Edomite—murdered the descendants of Esau's twin brother, Jacob and his wife, Rachel, by slaughtering all the innocent baby boys in Bethlehem.

Only I escaped.

12

Stepdad Settles In Sin City

BECAUSE OF THE ANGEL'S WARNING, we had fled from our house under cover of darkness and walked about three hundred miles across the desert and over the border into Egypt before my stepfather felt we were safe. It took us over two weeks and the trek was long and hard because of the rough terrain.

Fortunately, we had the gold and valuable spices from the astrologers. We were able to sell them to buy what we needed along the way. My father had plenty left over to rent a house and set up his shop when we found a safe village where nobody would recognize us.

Since Egypt was mainly desert, almost everyone lived in mud houses right along the banks of the massive Nile River. Because of the Nile, people were able to grow crops and live comfortably due to its life-giving waters; but only a few hundred yards out from the river on either side, there was totally barren desert for hundreds of miles. The Nile was the only thing that kept people alive. They rode up and down its waters on barges with their merchandise and only ventured into the deserts on the backs of camels when they had to leave the river.

Once we settled in our new land, my stepfather opened up a small carpentry business and my mother talked about having another baby. We started to make new friends and slowly integrated into the community. Like all Hebrews at that time, we spoke Aramaic at home. In Egypt we met people from many different tribes and languages in the market, and learned to eat the local food. We didn't tell anyone the real reason why we were there.

In the meantime, we waited to hear from God again as to when we could return home. Every now and again, a traveler passed by with news of what had happened in Bethlehem after we escaped, and how the families were coping. My mother missed her parents and wished we could go back home, but she realized that I had been the target of that deadly massacre and she was thankful to God that miraculously, my life had been spared.

Finally, one day when I was about six years old, the angel of the Lord appeared to my stepfather again in a dream.

"Get up, Joseph!" the angel said. "Take the young child and his mother and go back to the holy land of Israel, because King Herod has died a natural death and it's safe to return now." My stepfather was elated.

"Wake up, Mary! Wake up, Jesus!" he called to us excitedly. "I have good news! We can go back home now! King Herod is dead! We are free to leave!" This fulfilled the words of the prophet Hosea, who had predicted that God would call me to come out of Egypt.[67]

Our plan was to go right back to Bethlehem, my stepfather's home town. It would be another long walk lasting several weeks. We said our good-byes to the friends we had made in Egypt and took off.

However, when we crossed the border back into Israel, people told my stepfather alarming stories of what had been going on.

Stepdad Settles In Sin City

One evening I heard him talking about it in hushed tones with my mother when they thought I was asleep.

"I'm afraid to go back to Bethlehem and be so close to Jerusalem," he said. "Some of the travelers were telling me that things are very unstable now that King Herod the Great is dead. They said that the Romans divided his territories between three of his many sons. Herod Antipas got Galilee and Perea up north. His stepbrother, Philip, got the northeast regions. His brother, Archelaus, got the most important area. He's in charge of Judea, with the capital of Jerusalem, as well as Edom.

"The people I was talking to were from Jerusalem and they are terrified of Archelaus. They say he's really cruel. They said that there was a political uprising and he called in the Roman troops. The Roman soldiers butchered three thousand of our people right in the middle of the Passover festival. They crucified two thousand more! They stripped them naked, took them outside the city of Jerusalem and nailed them to crosses by the roadside as a warning for all to see."

"What shall we do, then?" my mother asked, terrified. She knew that crucifixion was the most horrific form of torture used by the Romans and she didn't want us to be in any danger.

"God spoke to me again in a dream and warned me not to go back," my stepfather replied, "and we really don't have to. We've already circumcised our son and presented him in the temple in Jerusalem, so he doesn't need to be near the capital. I think we should head back to Galilee instead. That way we can live close to your parents in Nazareth."

Galilee was in northern Israel, close to the border of Lebanon and not as strictly supervised by Rome. It was a beautiful area with rocky hills and mountains rising up to two thousand feet. The climate was pleasant and there was plenty of rainfall to fill the streams and waterfalls, which fed the fields of colorful wildflowers and watered the agricultural crops.

However, Nazareth, a village of about two hundred people, was not an ideal town for raising a family. Since it lay on the outskirts of the regional capital, Sepphoris, with merchants of all kinds traveling through, it had a reputation for immorality and lack of religion. But my grandparents, aunts, uncles and cousins all lived and worked there, so Nazareth was a natural alternative to Bethlehem. By settling there, the prediction came true that I would be called a Nazarene.

So we traveled north, avoiding the city of Jerusalem altogether. The walk back took a good three weeks. Of course, our relatives were all thrilled to meet me, and quickly helped us settle down. However, things weren't as safe as we had hoped.

"You need to keep a low profile," they urged us. "When news arrived that Herod the Great was dead, there was a rebellion up here as well, and the Romans pretty much destroyed Sepphoris. They even sold people into slavery. Things have been really tough, and work slowed down for a while. But everyone is focused on rebuilding Sepphoris now. We'll help you find work and raise your son."

13

Growing Up In Booming Suburb

AS THE YEARS IN NAZARETH went by, I grew up just like any other boy in our town. I helped my parents around the house and went grocery shopping with them to the big market in Sepphoris on weekends. The new governor, Herod Antipas, made a commitment to rebuild the city after the massacre, so there was plenty of construction work to keep our family busy.

On our frequent trips into Sepphoris, I saw exciting new building projects in full swing. Herod Antipas was moving quickly to rebuild the city. I watched the four thousand seat Roman auditorium being carved out of the hillside; a new palace, beautiful avenues flanked by large Roman columns, and several new religious halls for our people soon followed.

We didn't have any modern means of communication; we didn't even have electricity. After work we entertained ourselves with family and community events, all of which revolved around the holy books and the religious holidays that took place throughout the year.

As soon as I was old enough to be in elementary school, I studied reading, writing and arithmetic and memorized portions of God's holy books. The ancient scriptures were written in Hebrew, but we all spoke Aramaic, so I had to learn a new language. After elementary school, all the parents who could afford it would send their sons to train with one of the local religious teachers called rabbis. In Galilee, we had many fine teachers. They would accept a small group of students and then discuss the meaning of the ancient writings with them.

I loved being in my group. We wouldn't just sit in the classroom at the community center; we went out on field trips and asked our teacher all kinds of questions. Our teacher would discuss every aspect of life and God's holy books with us and then we would memorize the ancient texts word for word.

It had been a tradition for centuries to commit whole books to memory, and we practiced continuously to become more and more competent in reciting entire chapters at a time. Then our teacher would ask us many detailed questions and we had to be able to support our answers with the appropriate references.

Becoming an expert at understanding and discussing the holy books was the most important thing in every Hebrew boy's life. It prepared us to be knowledgeable and intelligent members of Hebrew society. We were as skilled with the words of the holy books as young people are with technology today!

Even the people who didn't go to school heard the holy books discussed and recited from memory in their homes and in their congregations. So much so, in fact, that as soon as someone quoted a few words, the people immediately recognized them and knew the rest of the text.

My parents also told me the ancient stories from the holy books as we went about our daily business or gathered for worship in our congregation. I helped my stepfather in the construction business and supported my mother and younger siblings who came along after me. As we worked together, my stepfather taught me about my world.

"The Romans believe that there are many different gods and goddesses," he told me. "Some of them are half god and half man, with one divine parent, and one human one. They also believe that spirits control different areas of the world. They build temples to these gods and fill them with treasures and statues of the gods in human form. When the people want to thank the gods, they bring animals to be sacrificed in the different temples by their priests," my stepfather told me.

"But we are Hebrews," he emphasized. "We are the only ones in the empire who proclaim that there is only one God, the God of Abraham, Isaac and Jacob. We refuse to bow down to anyone but the one true God. For centuries our people have been repeating the Shema prayer every morning and evening, saying these most critical words: 'Hear, O Israel: the Lord is our God, the Lord alone.' We want you to be a good son and learn all about our religious heritage, so that you too can obey the one true God."

I threw myself into my studies at school and at home and, little by little, I grew into a strong young man who knew the ancient writings very well. I loved God and God was good to me. My friends and family commented that I was unusually sensitive spiritually and exceptionally mature in my relationships. Those who loved me were pleased that I handled life so well for my age. They watched me grow steadily into manhood in the shelter of a safe and nurturing family.

Every night we gathered for dinner and my stepfather would bring news from the city.

"Governor Herod Antipas is really pushing the rebuilding projects. Nobody likes him because he's an Edomite, a descendant of Esau and not a descendant of Jacob, like we are. However, he has stabilized the area and kept our people here from rebelling against the Roman occupiers. We should be grateful for peace. I heard that his cruel elder brother, Archelaus, had another uprising in Jerusalem and this time, the Romans deposed him.

By the time I became a teenager, Governor Herod Antipas surprised us all by deciding to build a whole new capital about twenty miles away on Lake Galilee itself. Lake Galilee was the largest freshwater lake in the country; so big, in fact, that many people called it the Sea of Galilee. It was about thirteen miles long and eight miles wide.

The governor decided to name his new city Tiberias, after the reigning Roman emperor, Tiberius Caesar. Tiberius was known for his cruelty and his wildly immoral lifestyle, but Herod Antipas was focused on furthering his career by pleasing both Romans and Hebrews, just like his father had. As his entourage slowly began to leave Sepphoris for the new city, they reported back that Herod was supervising the construction of a new forum for the Romans, and a nice new religious assembly hall for the Hebrews. I was eager to see his luxurious new palace overlooking the glistening blue waters of the lake.

Yet another building rush was on, and I helped my stepfather build custom furniture in his workshop. We would deliver it to the wealthy people in the residential areas that were springing up all around the city, which gave me the opportunity to see the new construction going up.

When Herod Antipas finished his splendid new palace overlooking the lake, he asked the King of Petra in Jordan for his daughter's hand in marriage. Petra was the capital of the Nabatean kingdom—a desert area of dramatic canyons and narrow gorges, with magnificent temples and tombs carved out of the rose-red rock. For the princess, moving from the dry pink rocks of Petra to the lush green vegetation and beautiful lake palace in Tiberias was like moving to a lovely vacation resort.

Everyone was excited about the royal wedding and made preparations for a spectacular ceremony.

14

Frantic Search For Missing Boy

ALL GOOD HEBREW MEN WERE supposed to go up to Jerusalem for the three main religious festivals.[68] At Passover we remembered our ancestors' escape from slavery in Egypt and establishment as a nation. At Pentecost, we celebrated the giving of the law to Moses. During the Feast of Tabernacles we camped in tents for a week, to re-live what life was like during the wandering in the desert under Moses.[69] As time went by, my stepfather gradually began to feel comfortable about going back to Jerusalem and he promised that when the time was right, he would take me there too.

"Now that you are twelve years old," he announced on my twelfth birthday, "you have reached the official Hebrew age of manhood. You are old enough to go with us on our annual pilgrimage to the Passover festival this year."

This was a day I had been looking forward to for a long time as a student of the holy books and I was thrilled. I couldn't wait! Passover, the most important of the festivals, was always held in March or April. It was followed by a week-long holiday called the Feast of Unleavened Bread.

I was excited. I was going with my parents to a national convention for the very first time! We would have a whole week in the capital to enjoy the celebration.

"Will I get to see my cousin John when Uncle Zach and Aunt Beth come in from Hebron?" I asked.

"Of course you will, Son," Joseph said. "They live close to Jerusalem, but we have to walk about sixty five miles to get there. It's going to take us three or four days of hard walking uphill to reach the capital. I want you to exercise a lot so you can be fit for the journey. The ancient city of Jerusalem is our religious capital but it is off the beaten path. There are no trade routes passing through and no major rivers to carry us in by boat, so we have to walk. I think it's best for us to take the mountain route this year, to avoid Samaria."

The most direct route to Jerusalem went right through a forty-mile-long stretch of territory known as Samaria. It was an area of the country hated by all Hebrews. The Samaritans were old-fashioned Hebrews. They only read the first five of our holy books, and they did not go to the temple in Jerusalem for the festivals. They still worshiped on Mt. Gerizim, just like Abraham. They considered themselves more pure than the rest of us, but we considered them unclean and did not like to go through their territory.

"We can't afford to get contaminated by a Samaritan, even by accident," my stepfather said. "We would have to waste several days going through extra purification and a lot of money on lodging and additional sacrifices before we could participate in the Passover. It's just not worth it!"

"Centuries ago," my stepfather explained, "our ancestors in the north turned against God and welcomed wickedness. As punishment, God allowed the Assyrians from Iraq to ride in over our defenseless flatlands and conquer a large part of our territory.

"They deported many of our people into slavery in Iraq and brought in tribes from various parts of Iraq and Syria to populate and control the area. These foreigners worshiped pagan gods representing the sun and the moon, nature, fertility and many more.[70] They inter-married with the Hebrews that were left behind, and so now, we have a racial and religious melting pot called Samaritans."

The holy books said that we could not take part in any religious activity if we were ritually unclean. To become unclean, all we had to do was touch certain foods or a dead body. In addition, sexual relations, menstruation, childbirth,[71] marrying a non-Hebrew or accidentally touching a Samaritan automatically made us unclean.

"That's why many pilgrims traveling to Jerusalem chose to avoid Samaria altogether," my stepfather explained. "They prefer to take the alternate route through Jericho and then up the mountain pass to Jerusalem. It's a more dangerous route because sometimes there are robbers along the way; but we will be safe enough if we travel with our friends and relatives in a big group."

I couldn't wait for my first big trip! We packed, dropped my younger siblings off with relatives, and took off walking in a big convoy towards Jericho, which is eight hundred feet below sea level. I loved all the new smells as we walked through the lush tropical vegetation and past beautiful gardens.

"Jericho is one of the oldest cities in the world," my stepfather explained to the group as we walked. "King Herod the Great is the one who put it on the map and made it a place of international fame," he said. "I love to stop there on the way to Jerusalem."

Frantic Search For Missing Boy

My stepfather was considered very knowledgeable, so as soon as we found our lodgings, he led a group of us on a tour of the city. We walked past magnificent mansions with swimming pools, the fabulous civic center, the theater, and even the race track. We went to the market where merchants were milling around purchasing date palms and expensive medicines.

I was impressed.

The next day, we continued our climb up the mountain pass to Jerusalem, about twenty-five hundred feet above sea level. The air became dryer and dryer. The vegetation became more sparse as we climbed up the dry, dusty road.

"We have to stay with our group, Jesus, because there could be bandits hiding behind the rocks, and we don't want to be robbed," my stepfather reminded me. Fortunately, the journey passed without incident and by late afternoon we caught our first glimpse of the holy city. We stopped at a lookout point for a few minutes to enjoy the breathtaking view.

"See that enormous, eight-story building glistening in the sun?" my stepfather asked. "That's the new temple where your Uncle Zach worked," he said. "They've been doing construction on it for years now. See, it's built on a huge platform surrounded by those walls there. They say it's one of the biggest complexes in the Roman world!"

"That's right," said my mother. "It's an amazing building. You'll see. But you need to stay close to us. There are thousands of pilgrims coming in for the festival. The city will be very crowded and there will be Roman soldiers policing the streets and watching the temple from the fortress up there."

"You know, Son," my stepfather told me, "the Romans have forced all of their other conquered states to build temples to worship the Roman emperor, but our people refuse. We still travel to this temple to worship the one true God of Abraham, Isaac and Jacob. King Herod the Great, who died when you were a baby, built us this beautiful building and we continue to come here to sacrifice animals to God to pay for our sins, just as our ancestors did."

That week, I experienced my first visit to that awesome building—at least the first that I remember; I was just a baby when my parents brought me there for my dedication. The temple grounds were packed with pilgrims, their sacrificial lambs in tow. My stepfather took me through the Foreigners' Court, open to everyone, and past the Women's Court, where my mother joined the other women in worship.

My stepfather and I continued on to the central area—where only Hebrew men were allowed to enter. The priests were busy slaughtering the lambs and dashing their blood on the altar and burning their flesh. It was a scene of startling dramatic sights and pungent smells for a young small-town boy like me!

Even more interesting to me were the groups of people gathering around to hear the top religious leaders explain the holy books. I was fascinated. Every morning, when we arrived in the temple with our group of friends and relatives, I eagerly went to listen to their beautiful words of wisdom. The week flew by in interesting conversations as the teachers welcomed questions and comments from us as listeners.

Finally, when the last day's ceremonies were over, my parents started back to Nazareth, assuming that I was with some of our

Frantic Search For Missing Boy

traveling companions. They decided it would be quicker and easier to take the other, more direct, route home through Samaria. If they accidentally became contaminated, they would have plenty of time at home to become clean again. They had no idea that I was still in Jerusalem.

When my parents' caravan stopped to rest that first night, they looked for me among our friends and relatives but nobody had seen me. Nobody knew where I was. That's when they realized I was missing.

"We have to go back!" my stepfather told everyone. "If Jesus isn't with us, he has no idea where we are!" So he and my mother left the group and frantically headed back another day's journey to Jerusalem to look for me. They searched for me for a couple more days from morning till night, but with no success.

Finally, after three desperate days of looking and asking questions, they found me in the temple. I was with a group of scholars, listening carefully to their explanations and asking lots of questions. These scholars were so much more knowledgeable about the laws of God given to Moses than my teacher back in Galilee. When my parents saw me, they were relieved and surprised at the same time. My mother came running up to me.

"What's going on, Son?" she asked. "Why did you leave us and start acting so independently? Your stepfather and I have been worried sick. We've been looking for you everywhere for three whole days!"

"This young man is amazing," some of the people told my parents. "He's very intelligent and he has been asking lots of questions. We're very interested in the comments he's making. He seems to really understand the holy books!"

"Why did you come looking for me?" I asked my parents. "Didn't you know that I am now considered a man, and I work for my heavenly father?" My parents had no idea what I was talking about, but my mother sensed that it was significant.

"We have to go home, now, Son," my stepfather said. "Don't ever scare us like that again!"

Once we were reunited, I was happy to go back to Nazareth with my earthly parents and live under their guidance and authority. They said that I continued to grow in wisdom and learning and became more and more of a joy to God, to them and to my family and friends around me. The incident in the temple was not mentioned again, but I could tell from the way my mother looked at me from time to time, that she had not forgotten what I had told them that day.

15

Crowds Flock To Desert Preacher

SEVERAL MORE YEARS WENT BY and then, once again, something totally unexpected happened. One day, quite out of the blue, God spoke to my cousin John. By this time, John, Uncle Zach's miracle baby, was already a grown man. He was the tough, outdoor kind and spent most of his time alone in the wilderness.

John didn't look like ordinary city people. He wore rough clothes made of camel hair, tied together with a leather belt around his waist, and he hunted locusts for food. Our religion had very strict dietary laws, but locusts and even grasshoppers were allowed![72] He also liked to eat the honey he found in the desert.

John modeled his life after our ancient hero, Moses, who spent many years in the desert. One day Moses had been herding sheep when he noticed a bush that was on fire. He watched for a while, and, to his amazement, the flames kept getting higher and higher but the bush wasn't consumed! Moses was puzzled and went to take a closer look. All of a sudden, God called out to him and sent him on a mission to lead his people out of slavery in Egypt and to the Promised Land.[73]

My cousin had a similar experience to that of Moses. On that particular day, God stopped him in his tracks and sent him on a mission too. God called him to prepare the people of our day to enter a new promised land—not a physical land, but a spiritual experience of forgiveness and of freedom, starting on earth and continuing on to heaven itself. John's job was to let people know that I was on the way to be the Light of the world and to lead people out of spiritual darkness to a new freedom.

This all happened when the Emperor Tiberius was in the fifteenth year of his reign in Rome and Herod Antipas was still the Roman-appointed governor of Galilee. The new governor of Judea in the south, with its capital, Jerusalem, was now a Roman named Pontius Pilate.

After John's encounter with God in the desert, he was never the same again. On fire for God, he started preaching up and down the banks of the Jordan River to anyone who would listen. The first thing he did was to let the people know that I was on the way.

"He's the one I've been telling you about!" John explained to anyone who would listen. "He's coming behind me, but his rightful place is in front of me, because he existed long before I was born. We've received all kinds of wonderful blessings from him we don't even deserve, and he's coming to tell us about them. Reflect on your past and change your ways," he urged the people, "because God's spiritual community is closer than you realize!"

People started to call my cousin John the Baptist because he preached in the wilderness and baptized everyone who came to him looking for a fresh start in life. He did this by submerging their whole body into the Jordan River. The river was waist-deep in most places, which made it an ideal location for this symbolic ceremony.

Water baptism was an ancient tradition in our part of the world. Since the days of their desert wanderings, our people knew it as a ritual of bodily purification. But John gave it a much deeper meaning. The fresh running river water that flowed through the desert was considered a source of life. John said that it symbolically washed away their past, with all the bad things they had done. That is why John baptized them in the flowing waters of the river, and not in the stagnant waters of a pond.

"Look back over your lives and reflect on your past moral failures," John told the people. "If you see that you have done wrong, reconsider your options. Change your minds and choose a different way of being. Understand that the consequences of your bad decisions are always negative.

"Only if you walk away from your old habits, and don't look back and yearn for them, can you ever experience forgiveness and be released from the power of sin. Don't be like Lot's wife. When God rescued her family from the wicked cities of Sodom and Gomorrah, he instructed them not to look back. But Lot's wife heard the noise of destruction behind her so she stopped to watch the city going up in flames. God punished her disobedience by turning her into a pillar of salt, where she stands to this day.[74]

"So make the decision to leave your old lifestyle and never look back. Live only by looking forward into your new vision of yourself. Then show your inward commitment to change by going through the symbolic outward cleansing of the waters of baptism."

People flocked to John from all over Judea and Jerusalem and from all the settlements along the Jordan. They publicly confessed that they had failed to live up to God's standards and made the decision to change their lifestyle and live a life of purity.

That's when John submerged them in the river to symbolically wash away their sins so they could begin their new life with a clean conscience.

The people were so impressed with John that they wondered if he could be the ancient prophet Elijah who was supposed to come back to life.[75] Elijah had conclusively proved to the worshippers of the pagan god, Baal, that only God has real power. Elijah never died, but was taken up to heaven in a chariot of fire drawn by horses of fire and carried by a whirlwind. There were predictions saying that Elijah would return to earth some day.[76] John looked like Elijah, dressed like Elijah, and lived like a wild man in the desert, just like Elijah. *Was it possible,* the people wondered, *that John was Elijah come back to life?*

16

Rivals Pack Outdoor Auditorium

AS WORD OF MY COUSIN John's activities spread, members of the most prominent religious societies started coming to him to be immersed in the waters of the Jordan River as a sign that they were ready to give up their wicked ways.

During that time there were many religious societies. Three in particular stood out above the rest. They were the Desert Dwellers, the Spiritual Ones and the Realists.

The Desert Dwellers were the monks of our day. They were called Essenes. They were generally unmarried and lived a simple life in isolated settlements, where they shared everything in common. They devoted themselves to the study of the laws given by God to Moses and had very strict rules of obedience. In order to join them and be baptized into their group, you had to prove you were already living a holy life. However, they kept to themselves and didn't share their beliefs with outsiders at all. They stayed in their communes and didn't participate in the temple life in Jerusalem like the rest of us.

Some people thought that my cousin John was a member of the Desert Dwellers, but his message had a very different ring. He didn't call people to give up their lives and go wait for the end of the world in a remote desert community. Instead, he told them to change their lives and go back home to put their new behavior in practice right where they had previously failed.

The other two religious societies were much more prominent, especially the Spiritual Ones. They were spiritual because they believed in the supernatural. They totally accepted the miraculous powers of God and believed in angels and demons and life after death.

The Spiritual Ones were the most respected and the most influential religious leaders in the eyes of the common people. They were totally devoted to following God's laws despite the Roman occupation and were willing to die rather than give up the practice of their beliefs. They fearlessly stood up for our national identity and wore impressive religious outfits to attract attention to themselves. They were so particular about each and every detail of the law that over time, they developed over six hundred of their own rules and regulations to make sure that they kept the law.

The Spiritual Ones interpreted the complex religious law for the people, helping them put it into practice in their everyday lives. Even though they did not demand that others follow all their extra rules, they often came across as holier than everyone else and were resented by less strict believers. Their official name was Pharisees, and unfortunately, despite their devotion to God, their legalistic attitude ended up giving them a bad reputation.

The third group was the Realists. They considered themselves extremely practical. They believed that life here on earth is all we have. "If you see it," they taught, "then deal with it according to God's laws. If you don't see it—it doesn't exist!"

The Realists didn't believe in angels, or demons, or life after death. They believed in observing only what was written in the holy books without any of the interpretations of the Spiritual Ones. They overlooked all references to signs, wonders and supernatural beings in the holy books and didn't believe there was any life after death. They were officially called the Sadducees.

Most of the Realists were wealthy and came from the upper class. Many were traditional landowners who didn't want any political upsets that would cost them economic losses—so they did their best to get along with the Romans. After all, the Realists were practical; they knew the Romans had the power, so they were careful not to provoke them. The Roman rulers generally favored the Realists, but the common people didn't care for them at all.

"You hypocrites!" John growled at the Spiritual Ones and the Realists who were coming to him to be baptized. "Who warned *you* to escape the judgment of God? You believe that baby vipers chew through their mother's body to be born. You are just like them. You would destroy your own mothers to get what you want. You say you've given up your wicked lifestyles and want to be baptized? Let's see if you have really changed."

The Spiritual Ones and Realists looked at him in horror. In our culture, people had great love and admiration for motherhood. John's words cut through them like a knife.

"The prophet Malachi warned that if you do not repent and show proof of a good life," John continued unafraid, "you will be treated just like a dead tree. You will be burned to ashes, like a log burned in an oven, leaving neither roots nor branches.[77] You are like useless barren fruit trees, with no practical results to show for all your spirituality, and the axe is already lying on the ground next to your roots, ready to chop you up for firewood!

"Don't even think that you can escape God's punishment by claiming that you are descendants of Abraham—because God has the power to raise up children of Abraham out of the stones in this riverbed!"

"Do something useful. If you have two coats in your closet, give one away to someone who doesn't have a coat at all. If you have food in the house, do the same thing—share it with those who have nothing to eat. Don't just talk about spirituality. Do something good!"

"What should *we* do, Teacher?" asked the tax-collectors.

"Just be accurate when you collect the taxes," John replied.

Some soldiers came forward demanding to know what they should do.

"Don't steal. Don't cheat.[78] Don't use your position of strength and superiority to demand money from anyone. Don't threaten to beat people up if they don't do what you say. Don't take advantage of your power to accuse people falsely. Just do what the holy books say—don't lie and don't listen to gossip.[79] And lastly—be content with your wages."

John was causing such a stir that the Spiritual Ones in Jerusalem sent some priests who worked in the temple with Uncle Zach to ask him if he was the Savior.

"No, I'm not," said John. "I'm here to immerse you in water. I'm just the Messenger sent to prepare the way.

"Remember that the Savior will suddenly come to the temple. And who will survive the day of his coming? Who will stand when he appears? He is like the flame that a jeweler uses to purify gold to remove its impurities. He is like the soap you use to launder your clothes when you stomp on them with your feet and beat them in cold water to make them clean.[80]

"The Savior is on his way. When he comes, he'll invite those of you who are living good lives—producing good results and sharing God's way of life with others—to be a part of his eternal community in heaven.

"He's like a farmer at harvest time, who chops down everything in the field and then sorts the useful grain from the worthless straw and chaff. He will gather up the precious wheat and store it in his barn; but he'll throw the straw and chaff into the eternal flames. If you've done nothing for God, it will be very clear and evident for all to see and he'll leave you to burn in hell.

"The Savior is much greater than I am," John continued, "and he's already among you, even though you don't know it. He's right behind me, but he's much stronger than I am. I'm not even qualified to be his personal servant and bend down to take off his sandals. I have immersed you in water, symbolizing your cleansing from evil; but he will immerse you in the consuming fire of God that burns away all impurities. Then your children will speak God's words; your elders will dream about God; and your youth will see visions of God."[81]

The delegation from Jerusalem was not convinced.

"Well, if you're not the Savior," they asked John, "then who are you? Are you Elijah?"

"No, I'm not."

"Well then you must be the one called the Great Prophet!" they said. "We've read that God will raise up a prophet just like Moses. God will put words in his mouth and he will tell the people everything that God has commanded him to say; and the people will listen to him.[82] Are you the Great Prophet?"

"No, I'm not."

"Well then, tell us who you are so we can take an answer back to our people! What do you say about yourself?"

"I am the voice of one crying out to make a straight pathway in the wilderness, just like when we smooth out the roads when a king is on his way!" John said.[83] But they didn't understand.

"If you're not the Savior, and you're not Elijah, and you're not the Great Prophet, what are you doing baptizing people?" the Spiritual Ones wanted to know.

"I am a witness to God's Ray of Light," John answered, "so that you can all believe him because of me. I am not the light; but I am announcing that the Light of God—who shines into every man's world—is here!"

17

The Voice In the Sky

ONE DAY, I LEFT MY family home in Nazareth and made a pilgrimage to the Jordan River to be baptized by my cousin, John. I had been living with my parents all this time and everyone thought that my stepfather, Joseph, was my real father, and that my parents' other children were my real brothers and sisters. My half-brothers and sisters connected their ancestry through Joseph all the way back through King David to Abraham, Noah, and Adam, the first man in the Garden of Eden; but I traced my ancestry directly back to God, my heavenly father.

When I arrived at the banks of the Jordan I found John there, busy baptizing people. In fact, I got there the day after he had been questioned by the delegation from Jerusalem. When he saw me coming towards him, he stopped what he was doing, looked at me and announced:

"Here he is! God's perfect lamb! He is the one who will pay for the sins of all the people in the world!"

That was a stunning statement, because the Hebrews immediately knew that John was referring to the Passover lamb. Every year, at Passover, all our family members would gather to re-enact the special meal our ancestors had eaten the night before they escaped from Egypt. It was called the Passover meal. At that meal, we would recount how our ancestors had been slaves in Egypt and how God had told them to cluster in families and eat that last supper together.

The centerpiece of the dinner had to be a one-year-old male lamb or goat without defect or blemish. It became known as the Passover Lamb.[84] Egyptians did not eat sheep and they did not kill sheep. They worshiped sheep. Massive statues of their male ram-god, called Ammon-Ra, with his large rounded horns, were everywhere in their grand stone temples and palaces. Ammon-Ra symbolized male virility and strength in battle. So when God ordered our ancestors to kill and eat a lamb in our month of Nisan, on the night of the full moon, which was the height of the celebrations in the Egyptian Month of the Ram, he was directly challenging the Egyptians, their ability to have many children, and their military power in the region.

On that first Passover night, our Hebrew ancestors, who were all powerless slaves of the Egyptians, took the risk and obeyed God. They slaughtered their Passover lambs and gathered in families for their last supper, believing that Moses would lead them out of Egypt the following day. Small families joined with their neighbors. A delicious hot meal would give them strength for the long journey ahead. They were to eat the meal fully clothed and in a hurry, ready to walk out the door at a moment's notice. As they ate the lamb, they all realized they were demolishing the symbol of Egyptian power.

Then they were to take the lamb's blood and smear it on the doorposts of their houses as a public sign of their allegiance to the one true God. As they did so, they all knew they were directly defying Egyptian beliefs and risking their lives to do so.

The Voice In the Sky

After they had all gone to bed, God sent the angel of death to punish the Egyptians for mistreating the Hebrews for all those years. The angel entered every house not marked with blood, and killed the first-born son, as well as the first-born family pet and beast of burden; but wherever he saw the blood of the Passover lamb on the door, he kept right on going past that house, sparing that family from death.

I remember how every year, ever since I was a little boy, we looked forward to celebrating Passover. Every year, I went with my stepfather to select a little male lamb without spot or blemish. We had to keep it close to the house for four days, to make sure it was perfect in every way. We liked to spend a lot of time with the lamb, holding it, petting it and looking it over from head to toe. It was so sweet and defenseless, and of course, we always fell in love with it.

Even as we bonded with our own little lamb, we knew that our precious pet was destined to pay for everything we had done wrong that year. We were always sad to lose our baby lamb, but so grateful that it was taking our place, so that we would not have to pay the death penalty for our own sins.

When the people at the Jordan River heard John call me the Passover lamb, they knew exactly what that meant. They remembered that the prophet Isaiah wrote about a man who would be brought as a lamb to the slaughter. He would be as quiet as a sheep in the hands of its shearer and go to his death without protest, just like the Passover lamb.[85]

John was telling them clearly that I would one day be sacrificed, like the Passover lamb, to pay for the sins of every man and woman, and every boy and girl and teenager, in every age and every culture. Those who obeyed would absorb what I said and did, and have strength for life's journey. Those who publicly declared their allegiance to God would be spared from his deadly judgment.

"He's the one I've been telling you about all this time," John said, pointing to me. "I told you that someone much greater than I is coming! I had no idea who it would be, but I knew that one day he would appear. The whole reason I came to the Jordan to baptize you was to prepare you for this moment—and here he is!"

I climbed down the riverbank and started to wade through the water towards John.

"Why are you coming to be baptized by me?" John protested. "I need to be immersed by you, not the other way around, because I know now that you existed long before I did."

"It's the right thing to do," I insisted.

My cousin obeyed and submerged me in the river. At the very moment when I came up out of the water and opened my eyes, I saw the sky open. God's Spirit came down on me in the physical shape of a dove. As soon as the dove settled on me, we all heard a voice from heaven saying:

"This is my precious son. I am so very pleased with him."

For centuries God had promised to send his son to be the Savior.[86] This son would be a mirror-image of his father. He would not yell or be aggressive like a ruthless invader; he would not crush the down-trodden like a powerful ruler; he would not hurt the sick and dying like an unfeeling conqueror. Instead, he would open blind eyes to the wonder of God and gently bring those suffering from emotional anguish out from their prisons of spiritual ignorance and abuse.[87]

"I saw the Spirit myself," John reported later. "The Spirit came down from heaven like a dove. I didn't know who the Savior would be; but the Spirit of God who sent me out to the Jordan to baptize with water had prepared me, saying: 'When you see the Spirit descending and remaining on this one specific person, then you will know precisely who it is that immerses people in the Spirit of God.' I had no idea it would be my cousin, Jesus; but now there is no doubt in my mind that he is the Son of God."

That day marked the start of my public service to God as his son on earth. I was thirty years old.

18

Evil Lurks In Desert Boot Camp

WHEN I EMERGED FROM THE water I was full of the Spirit of God. As soon as I started wading back out of the river, I felt the Spirit pull me away from everyone and drive me deep into the wilderness, alone. God's plan was to prepare me for the mission ahead by bringing me face to face with the devil in my own personal boot camp.

As I walked along in the desert, the sun beat down on me by day. The bitter cold chilled me to the bone at night when I burrowed a sleeping hole for myself in the sand. The area was desolate and home to many kinds of dangerous wild animals—poisonous snakes and wild beasts constantly on the prowl for something to eat.

Even though I could have helped myself to locusts and honey, I decided to fast for forty days and forty nights, just like Moses and Elijah before me. By the time my full forty days and nights of fasting were up, I was starving.

You might think that I was alone in the desert, but I wasn't. Someone was watching me. Satan, whose name means adversary, or opponent, had been carefully observing my every move, waiting for my moment of weakness. When Satan saw how hungry and exhausted I was, he made a desperate attempt to push me to sin.

"If you really are the son of God," he proposed, "why don't you speak to this stone here and tell it to miraculously transform into a loaf of bread, so that you can eat and satisfy the hunger pains in your stomach?"

Satan was trying to get me to use my heavenly abilities to do something to opt out of human suffering. He wanted me to break down and comfort myself by meeting the needs of my physical body with physical food. Unlike the rest of humanity, I would then be able to get out of suffering whenever circumstances became too uncomfortable.

But I understood that I was God's sacrificial lamb. I knew that my mission was to fully live the life of a human, with all the trials and temptations that entails, and ultimately to suffer and die so that mankind could be saved from God's judgment against sin. If Satan could convince me to opt out of suffering, he would cause me to opt out of being the sacrifice.

What's more, if he could taunt me into turning the stone into bread, the masses would eagerly follow me just because I could provide free food. Satan wanted me to earn instant popularity by bribing people with material gifts! But that was not what my mission was about either. People are not animals. They are created in the image of God and my mission was to let people know that there is a higher calling and a higher purpose than just meeting our material needs.

I knew exactly what Satan was trying to do and I refused to fall into his trap. I counteracted at once by quoting the holy books, which I had memorized for just such a time as this.

"It is written," I said to Satan, "that God, who led the Hebrew people out of Egypt and into the desert to experience hunger, also provided delicious honey bread called manna for them to eat. He taught them that people need more than just physical food and medicine to be healed and energized. Real energy and healing come from absorbing every word of God and every divine revelation that comes from him.[88] God's word is to the spirit of man what food is to his body."

"Satan," I said resolutely, "I told you to go away! God's words are my food and I won't let you manipulate me!"

But Satan would not give up. Instead, he personally escorted me up to the top of a high mountain. From there, he showed me all the countries of the world in all their splendor and attractiveness.

"I am the prince of this world," he said boastfully. "I have been given the power to reign over all the nations, and I have the right to give that power to whomever I desire." This was true.

"Because I have this right, I would be willing to give you the power to rule over all these lands and to enjoy all their benefits. All you have to do is bow down and adore me and everything will be yours. What could be easier? Just obey me and do everything I tell you to do—and it will all be yours! Then all the people in the world will have to obey you!"

Satan hadn't totally succeeded in his own rebellion against God. Now he wanted nothing better than to have me, the Son of God, fall at his feet. Giving away the world would be a small price to pay.

"Go away, Satan!" I said. "Get out of here! I will not bow down to you! The holy books clearly state that God is the creator of the universe and he is far above you. He owns the world and he is the only one we should reverence and fear. He is the only one we should be devoted to and serve with all our hearts.[89] He is the only one we should cling to and identify with.[90] He is awesome, and we should serve him with all sincerity, because serving him is a wonderful and exciting experience, and I don't need to have any possessions in order to fulfill my mission!"

Satan heard everything I said, but still, he didn't give up. He came back to attack me yet a third time. This time, he took me up to the holy city of Jerusalem and he set me high up on the rooftop of the tallest building in the temple grounds.

"If you really are the Son of God," he challenged, "why don't you just jump? You're so determined to quote the holy books. Don't you remember that God promised to order his angels to look after you and carry you in the palms of their hands, so you never even stub your toe on a stone?[91] So jump! Prove to me that they'll catch you! Go on! Do it!"

Satan knew that the people were expecting the Savior to appear in the temple. If I caused a sensation, he reasoned, I could forget my true mission. Satan had figured out that I was combating him using the very words of God. Being the schemer that he is, he decided to use that same tactic against me. He was not ignorant of the holy books; he was just as able to quote their passages as I was.

"If you throw yourself off the pinnacle here in the holy temple in Jerusalem in front of crowds of people, and if they see that you miraculously survive the fall, you'll be an instant celebrity!" he reasoned. I wouldn't have to bother using my miraculous powers for the good of humanity. I could just use them to draw attention to myself as a heavenly being and people would be in awe of me.

However, I knew that being famous wouldn't resolve the people's predicament of guilt before God. Satan's proposal seemed flashy. It seemed easy. But I knew that he was just trying to get me to take my eyes off my mission. He wanted to trick me into believing that I could succeed by doing things his way instead of God's.

"Look Satan," I said firmly, "the holy books say that we must not provoke God, nor make him prove himself by testing him![92] We are supposed to be faithful to him and trust him and put away all false gods.[93] I don't need to be sensational in order to fulfill my mission. I am not interested in any of your so-called brilliant ideas, so just leave!"

When Satan finally saw that each time he had tempted me I had won by quoting the holy passages, he decided to leave me alone. He was sure he could find another opportunity to defeat me another day, using a different tactic.

As soon as Satan left, angels came to my side to help and encourage me. I had passed the test and it was time to break the fast and head back to civilization.

19

Two Recruits Argue

THE DAY AFTER I GOT back to the Jordan River, I noticed that my cousin John was there with a couple of his friends. Just as he was getting up to preach, he saw me walking by.

"Look, there's God's lamb again!" John said to his friends. They immediately took off after me.

"Can I help you?" I asked them.

"Yes, Sir," said one of them. "My name is Andrew. We are followers of John. We were here when John called you God's lamb on the day of your baptism, and we are curious. We want to know more... Can you tell us where you are staying?"

"Come and see," I said. "You're welcome to spend the night with us; it's getting late."

Andrew was excited and ran immediately to get his brother, Simon, to join us also.

"Hey, Simon!" he said. "My friend and I have found the Savior and he has agreed to talk to us! Hurry!" Simon dropped what he was doing and rushed out the door with his brother.

"So you are Simon, son of Jonah?" I said, when Andrew introduced him. "From now on, I'm going to call you Cephas in Aramaic, and Peter in Greek, because it means 'a stone.'"

The men spent the night and we talked until late over dinner. The following day we took a walk along the shore of Lake Galilee, where we ran into their friend, Philip.

"Come join me," I said to Philip. "I want you to be on my team."

"Great," said Philip, "but can I go and get my friend Nate, so he can come too?"

"Of course," I said. So Philip went to look for Nathaniel.

"Hey, Nate," he said. "You won't believe what just happened! We've found the Savior! His name is Jesus. He's the son of Joseph, and he's from Nazareth."

"Nazareth?" exclaimed Nate in disgust. "The prophet Micah wrote that the Savior is supposed to come from Bethlehem in Judea—not Nazareth in Galilee! That's miles away! You're way off! How can anything good come from Nazareth? I should know. I'm from the highlands of Cana, just down the road from there! We all know what a bad reputation Nazareth has!"[94]

Undeterred, Philip said, "Yes, I know, but come anyway, and check him out for yourself!"

"Look, everyone," I said when Nate arrived. "Nate is a true Hebrew, genuine and above deceit.[95] God will bless people like him, because he isn't a hypocrite who just talks to please people. No. He is accurate and gets his facts right."[96]

"Where do you know me from?" Nate asked, puzzled.

"I noticed you earlier, back when you were studying under the fig tree," I said.

"Wow!" exclaimed Nate. "I thought you were a respected teacher, but now I see that you know me inside out! You are obviously the Son of God and King of Israel!"

Two Recruits Argue

"Nate," I said, "You trust me because I knew exactly what you're like from a distance. Well, you're going to see much greater things than these. Do you remember how our ancestor, Jacob, dreamed that he saw the angels of God going up and down a ladder all the way up to heaven?[97] You too will see heaven open up and the angels of God ascending and descending on me, just like they did in Jacob's dream," I promised.

20

Wedding Caterers Caught By Surprise

THREE DAYS AFTER I MET Nate, he invited my mother and me to a wedding in his home town of Cana, just a few miles from our house. I took my small group of followers with me and we mingled with the guests, enjoying the celebrations. There were a lot of people there and my mother noticed that there wasn't enough wine for everyone. She was concerned and decided to bring it to my attention.

"Look, Son," she said, "they've run out of wine already!"

"That's not our problem, Ma'am," I said, addressing her formally in public. "It's too early for me to make a move."

She didn't pay any attention to what I said. Instead she went right up to the caterers and said: "If my son tells you to do something, just do it!"

They had six large stone pots used to hold water for our ceremonial washings, called ablutions, that we performed before praying and eating. Each pot held about twenty-five gallons.

I went up to the caterers and told them to fill the pots with water. They hurried off to the well and carried back enough buckets of water to fill each pot to the brim. When they had finished, I told them to draw some out and take it to the master of ceremonies.

Wedding Caterers Caught By Surprise

When he tasted it, the water had miraculously turned into delicious wine. He couldn't explain where the wine had come from, so he called the bridegroom over.

"I'm impressed!" he said to the bridegroom. "Most people put out the good wine first, and then, once the guests have consumed so much that they're a little drunk and can't tell the difference, they bring out the cheaper wine. But you've kept the best for last!" Of course, the caterers knew what had happened, but they didn't say a word.

This was the beginning of my miracle ministry and the first time that I publicly revealed my inner power. When they saw that I had turned water into wine, my team members began to believe in me.

After the wedding celebrations, my mother, my half-brothers and half-sisters, and my small group of team members all went down to the relaxing town of Capernaum on the shores of Lake Galilee and stayed there for a few days.

21

Leader Sneaks In For Secret Talks

WHEN PASSOVER WEEK ROLLED around, I went up to Jerusalem for the festivities as usual. Because the city was up in the mountains, it was several days' walk uphill from Galilee. When I arrived, I settled into my lodgings and prepared to spend some time at the temple worshipping God and discussing the holy books with the learned teachers in the temple.

While I was in the city, I had the opportunity to perform a few miracles. Many of the bystanders believed in me right away, but I didn't trust them, because I knew what they were really like. People judge others by their clothes, their hairstyle, the softness of their skin, the size of their property, the number of servants and possessions they have, or what's in it for them; but God looks at the heart.[98] He has superior knowledge of everything that people are planning and thinking about,[99] and I knew that these people were not really ready to listen to me.

Late one night, after I got back in from the temple, there was a knock on my door. When I opened it, I recognized one of the religious leaders standing there in the shadows. He had obviously come to my lodgings under cover of night because he didn't want to be seen with me in public. I invited him in and we sat down to talk by candlelight. It turned out that he was a Spiritual One named Nicodemus.

"Sir," he confessed secretly, "we know that you're a teacher sent to us by God, because no one can perform the signs and miracles that you do, unless God is with him."

"You're right, Nick," I said. "In fact, unless a person is born again and receives the gift of God's Spirit, he can never experience or understand the presence and power of God in his heart."

"But how can a man be born when he's already fully grown?" Nick asked. "Surely, he can't climb back into his mother's womb and be born all over again?"

"Listen, Nick," I explained, "I'm not talking about physical birth! Unless your spirit is born of water and the life-saving Spirit of God, you can't be a part of God's spiritual community. Physical things are born physically, but spiritual things are born spiritually.

"Don't look so amazed when I say you have to be born again! Just consider the wind. On a windy day you can see the trees moving and you can hear the wind howling; but you don't know where the wind came from, nor where it's going. The same thing happens in the spiritual realm with everyone who has been born of God's Spirit. That Spirit moves wherever he wants to move. You don't know where he came from, nor where he's going, but you can see the evidence of his presence in people's lives."

"I don't understand," said Nick, perplexed.

"Here you are," I continued, "a Spiritual One who supposedly believes in the supernatural! You're a respected teacher of the people, yet you don't seem to understand the basics about God! Trust me—I'm telling you what I know for a fact, and I'm sharing with you what I have personally seen in heaven. But you don't believe me.

"If you don't believe me when I explain how things happen here on earth, how will you possibly trust me when I tell you about heaven? No human being has ever gone up to heaven, but I have. I live in heaven, and I've come down from heaven to show you what life is like up there.

"Let me give you a comparison, Nick. You remember how Moses lifted up the brass serpent in the wilderness, when our ancestors were fleeing from Egypt? God instructed Moses to make that serpent out of brass and put it on a pole.[100] Then whenever people were bitten by a real snake while crossing the desert, all they had to do was look at the brass serpent on the pole, and they lived.

"This is exactly what will happen with me," I continued. "I am God's humble servant, and I must be lifted up on a pole so that if people look at me and trust me, they will be saved from eternal punishment and destruction. Instead of judgment, they'll have constant, vibrant and never-ending spiritual life!

"You know, Nick, God loves this beautiful world and all the people in it so much that he has offered me—his precious only child—to the world as a gift. His reason? If anyone, anywhere in the world, in any age and any culture, entrusts his life to me, that person will not be lost or destroyed for eternity in hell. Instead, he or she will have an abundant, rich and full life that starts now and goes on and on, forever and ever."

Nick leaned forward. He was starting to understand.

"God didn't send me here to judge and condemn people, Nick. On the contrary, he sent me here to serve you and to save you! If you trust me as God's only son—you are not judged or condemned; but if you don't trust me—you are condemned already, because you don't believe in me and in the mission that I have been sent to accomplish.

"I am God's Light, which makes everything visible. I've come to make things crystal clear for people; and yet some choose to live in darkness. They actually love the darkness more than the light, because most of their actions are evil. You see, people who do bad things hate God's light. They especially don't want to come to me, because I am the Light. They are terrified that the evil they have done might be discovered and they will be exposed!

"Some people are stubborn and resist God's exposing light. They don't want to understand and they don't want to follow his lifestyle. The light is shocking and intrusive—the end of their partying and the death of their dreams. They live in deep darkness and terror. Their lives are full of internal anguish and constant trouble. Daily, they experience the fallout of death![101] They are guilty of judgment.

"On the other hand, people who live sincere and truthful lives gladly come to my light, so that their actions may be seen publicly and recognized as works of God. Those kinds of people give God the credit for every good thing they do."

Nick, the Spiritual One, left my lodgings that night with a lot to think about. His life would never be the same.

22

Secrets to Effective Prayer

AT THE END OF THE Passover celebrations, I left Jerusalem and rejoined my team just outside the city. We found a place to stay in the southern area of Judea, and spent time talking together. They were progressing well, learning from me and putting my teachings into practice.

"Sir," said one of them in a concerned tone. "Your cousin John is baptizing hundreds of people in the Jordan River and teaching them how to pray. Now that people are coming to you for baptism, would you please teach us how you pray?"

"Of course," I replied. "Here is what not to do: when you pray, don't be like the religious hypocrites. They go through their self-righteous routine like actors on stage. They love to be seen in their religious groups or out in public so that everyone will think of them as shining examples of spirituality! Here is the problem with that. They get instant gratification from being seen and admired right there and then, but that is all the reward they will ever get.

"Here is what you should do: when you want to ask God for something good, or when you need his help to avert some danger or evil, find a quiet room with complete privacy. Go inside and close the door, so nobody can see you.

"Remember how God's prophet Elisha went up privately to pray for the widow's son who died? He closed the door behind him and begged God for the life of the boy. God heard his secret prayer and brought the dead boy back to life. Then everyone got to see the result, but not while Elisha was talking to God about his request.[102] So speak to God when nobody is watching, and he will reward you publicly.

"Here's something else you should keep in mind when you pray. Tell God clearly what you want and why you are praying. Don't just ramble on and on like ignorant people do. They think that the longer they pray, and the more they repeat themselves, the more likely they are to be heard. That is not true. The holy books say that your words should be few.[103]

"Remember how the followers of the pagan god Baal called on him for a miracle from early morning until evening and nothing happened? On the other hand, the prophet Elijah simply said: 'True God, hear me,' and instantly fire fell from heaven in answer to his prayer?[104] God already knows what you need from him before you ask, so pray like this:

"Dear Father in heaven, we love you and thank you for who you are. We want everyone in the world to be a part of your community of love and we're willing to help you achieve that. We're eager to carry out your wishes here on earth with the same precision and perfection with which they are carried out by your angels. They listen carefully to your voice and love to do whatever you ask.[105] As your devoted subjects, we are willing to do the same.

"Please give us our daily bread,[106] the words of wisdom, instruction and encouragement that we need to sustain our lives here on earth today, for they are more valuable than food.[107]

"Free us from the guilt of our past and the power it holds over us. Forgive us the debt payment we owe you for the evil we have done. We in turn, agree to forgive those who have done us wrong. We agree to release everyone from any moral or personal obligation to repay us, and we free them from their guilt.

"Please don't lead us into the path of testing and temptation. Instead, drag us forcefully out of the path of pain, sorrow, labor, wickedness and mischief, because you have the power and the royal dominion and the glory now, and you always will. All greatness, power, glory, victory, majesty and sovereignty belong to you, God.[108] Amen.

"If you pray like this, then God will hear you." My team members looked delighted that I made it so simple, but I had a stern warning for them.

"Never forget," I said, "how important it is to forgive people when they hurt you, whether they do it on purpose, or unknowingly. It is important to let that memory and that pain go, and not retaliate or demand that they make it up to you. If you do that, then your heavenly father will do the exact same thing for you. But if you don't let go of the hurt and blame when others fail you, your heavenly father will not overlook your failings either. He will treat you just like you treat them. If you don't forgive them, he won't forgive you!"

My team members looked shocked, and I knew that they needed a lot of practice.

"When you pray," I reminded them, "always ask God to guide you, and he will. Even though you are a mere human, and God is so much greater than you, when you ask him for something, he'll grant your request. He is the one who said, 'When you cry out to me and pray to me, I will hear you. You'll seek me and find me when you search for me with all your heart.'[109]

"I promise you that if you turn to God and sincerely look to discover who he is, you will find him. If you knock on God's door, he will open it and welcome you in because God is passionately in love with those who love him,[110] and wants to have an intimate relationship with every person in the world. Everyone who asks God for something will receive his request. Everyone who sincerely looks for God will find him. Everyone who knocks on his door will see the door opened for him.

"Why does God do that?" asked one of my followers.

"That's a good question," I said. "Let's pretend that you show up at your good friend's front door at midnight and start banging on the door. Nothing happens, so you start yelling. 'Hey there, I need to borrow three loaves of bread!' you shout. 'Some guests from out of town dropped in unexpectedly. They are spending the night with us, but I have no food and all the grocery stores are closed for the night!'

"Your friend will probably want to say, 'Look, I'm sorry. I can't get up and help you now. I've already locked my front door. The kids are all in bed with me. The animals are all lying down inside the house. Don't bother me now! I can't get up, because I'd disturb everyone and it would take a while to get them all to settle back down again.'

"The point of my illustration is this: your friend will not get out of bed because he's your friend; but he will get up if you keep making a racket until he answers the door. He may not want to get up, but he will if you are bold enough to disregard the rules of polite society and insist on his help. He will get up, light a candle, wake all the children and animals, open the door and give you whatever you need.

"If your friend is willing to give you what you need just because you pester him, how much more do you think that God is willing to bless you, just because you ask?

"So I say: ask, and you will receive. Keep looking and you will find what you need. Knock, and the door will be opened for you. Because if you ask, you will receive; if you keep looking, you will find what you need, and if you knock, the door will open for you."

23

Rivals Question Leadership

A FEW DAYS LATER, A MAN showed up, wanting me to baptize him. John's people argued with him and said no, John should do it.

"John!" his followers confronted my cousin. "You are our teacher and we respect you, but we have a problem. Do you remember the man you pointed out as God's lamb? Well, he's now baptizing too, and everyone is going out there to him! What do you have to say about that?"

They and the Spiritual Ones were convinced that I had more followers than John, and that I was baptizing more people than John, although my team members were actually doing most of the immersing.

"Look," said my cousin, "we each have a mission in life, and God is the one who gives it to us. I clearly stated that I am not the expected Savior, but that I am the Messenger sent ahead of him to announce his coming. You yourselves heard every word I said—remember?

"I'm sure you're familiar with the words of the prophet Malachi. He predicted that God would send his messenger to get people to clean up their lives, just like when people wash their clothes to be all dressed up for an upcoming celebration; but this time, they would be preparing themselves for the Savior.[111]

"Let me put it another way. Wouldn't you agree that the luckiest man at a wedding is the bridegroom—because he gets the bride—right? The best man stands beside him and is delighted for him, listening with great joy to what the groom has to say; but he is not the one who is at the center of the wedding ceremony—the groom is. It's the same here. Jesus is the bridegroom and I'm the best man. He must get more and more attention, while I must start fading into the background.

"You may think that Jesus is my cousin, and he is; but I know that he has come down from heaven," John explained, "and he is way above all of us. Like you, I'm human, so I speak about earthly things. Jesus, on the other hand, is from heaven. He keeps telling us what he has seen and heard in heaven and people just don't want to believe him. But those who do believe him believe God. Their faith acts like an official stamp of approval on a document, verifying that it is authentic and true.

"Jesus was sent to deliver God's powerful words to us. God has not held back or restrained his spirit in him at all. On the contrary, God the Father loves his son and has put everything in the universe at his disposal; the fullness of God's Spirit is in him and expressed by him," explained John.

"If you entrust yourself to God's Son, Jesus, and have confidence in his love and care," John continued, "you automatically have a vibrant and never-ending spiritual life. On the other hand, if you don't believe or obey him, you will not live to experience that quality of life now, or in the hereafter. Instead, God's anger and punishment are already present in your lives."

John made his message crystal clear and everyone who heard him was amazed at his words.

24

Royal Affair Rocks Palace

OUR GOVERNOR, HEROD ANTIPAS, had a half-brother, Philip, who lived in Italy with his beautiful wife, Herodias. On one of his visits to Rome, Governor Herod fell madly in love with Philip's wife. He used all his charms to win her over, and soon they were involved in an adulterous affair. Herod was determined to take Herodias back with him to Galilee. His strategy worked and Herodias agreed to leave Philip and marry him. Soon, she would be moving with him back to his lakeside palace in Tiberias, with her beautiful teenage daughter, Salome, in tow.

Meanwhile, Herod's wife, the Nabatean princess, was waiting for him back at the lakeside palace. When she heard that her husband was coming back with a new wife, she immediately escaped to Fort Machaerus in Jordan. From there, she fled through the gorges back to her father's capital of Petra, afraid of what Herod might do to her. By the time Herod and his new wife returned to Tiberias, she was gone.

When my cousin John heard what had happened, he publicly criticized the Governor.

"You're an adulterer!" John said to him. "You know that God's law says that you may not uncover the nakedness of your brother's wife.[112] Sleeping with Herodias is wrong and you'll be cursed with childlessness![113] You're a Hebrew, a descendant of

Abraham. You have been raised with the Ten Commandments! You should know better!"

On the one hand, King Herod was deeply disturbed by John's finger of accusation and really took his words to heart. On the other hand, he continued to listen to John's teachings with great eagerness and even followed many of his ways.

Herodias had no such concerns. She bitterly resented my cousin for meddling in their relationship and embarrassing her in public and she kept pressuring her new husband to have John killed. At times he wanted to, but he was afraid to do anything because the people considered John to be a prophet.

Herod solved his dilemma by putting John in prison instead. With John out of the public eye and out of harm's way, Herod didn't have to face the issue of executing him.

"Your cousin has been arrested!" my friends came to tell me one day. "He condemned Herod's adulterous marriage in public, and now he's in jail!"

During my infancy, King Herod the Great had tried to have me killed as a baby. Now his son, Herod Antipas, had my cousin behind prison bars.

"What's going to happen next?" people were asking themselves.

The situation did not look good for John at all.

25

Woman's Secret Past Revealed

I DIDN'T WANT TO BE involved in any controversy in the capital so I immediately left Judea and God's Spirit led me to start walking back north to Galilee via Samaria. As I went, I told everyone the good news that God's community was already forming here on earth, and word of my teachings spread throughout the countryside.

We walked all morning on our way through Samaria and arrived close to the town of Sychar. I was tired and wanted to take a break. On the outskirts of town was a piece of property that Abraham's grandson, Jacob, had bought for a hundred pieces of silver, after dreaming that he saw angels climbing up and down a ladder that stretched from heaven to that very spot on earth.[114]

As we passed by the property, I spotted Jacob's old well and went over to sit down on the rim to relax. The rest of my team continued on into town without me, so they could buy food for the group.

I was very thirsty, but there was no bucket there. Eventually, a Samaritan woman arrived at the well with a big pot that she was going to drop down into the well. I didn't move away to avoid her. Instead, I asked for her help.

"Excuse me," I said, "would you mind giving me a drink?"

"Aren't you a Hebrew?" she said, surprised. "I'm a Samaritan, and on top of that, I'm a woman! So what are you doing here, and why would you lower yourself to have a conversation with me? You people say that Jerusalem is the only correct place to worship God, but then you wouldn't let our people help you rebuild the temple in Jerusalem when you came back from your captivity in Babylon.

"That's why we had to build our own temple!" she said resentfully. "It's in ruins now, but we still gather for worship on the mountain tops. In fact, we still shout out the blessings of the one true God from the top of Mt. Gerizim; and the curses for disobeying him from the top of Mt. Ebal.[115]

"We even have hilltop shrines to many other gods that were brought in with the Assyrian invasion.[116] So we have plenty of religious activity everywhere. But why are you here? Why are you talking to me—even asking me for a favor?" she asked. I had a very simple answer:

"If you realized that I am a gift from God," I said, "you would ask *me* for a favor, and not the other way around! Then I would give you life-giving eternal water to drink, instead of the still, dead water from this well!"

"Where would you get that kind of living water, Sir?" she asked. "You don't even have a bucket, and this well here is very deep! This well belonged to Jacob, who drank its water and gave it to his children and cattle. We are his descendants, and we still drink from it. Are you more important than Jacob?"

"If you drink the water from this well," I responded, "you'll be thirsty again in a few hours. But if you drink the water that

Woman's Secret Past Revealed

I give you, you'll never be thirsty again – ever! My water is not stagnant water from the bottom of a cold well. It's like a fresh, sun-filled spring, bubbling up constantly and bringing everlasting life!

"The prophet Isaiah predicted that one day there would be wells of salvation and great joy," I explained.[117] "He promised that God would pour out his spirit like water on the thirsty,[118] and his blessings like floods on the dry ground to wash away all sin!"[119].

"Oh, I like that, Sir!" the woman exclaimed. "Give me this special water, so I don't ever have to be thirsty again—or have to carry those heavy pots home from the well every day!"

"All right," I said, "but first go and get your husband."

"I'm not married," the woman answered, a little embarrassed.

"I know you're not!" I replied. "And I appreciate your honesty. You see, I know that you've had five husbands, and the man you're currently living with is not your husband!"

"Oh, my God," said the woman, "you must be a prophet, or how else would you know all that about me?"

"Believe me," I told her, "you Samaritans don't even know who you worship. We do, because the salvation of the world comes through the Hebrew people. But very soon people won't have to worship God on Mt. Gerizim, or in Jerusalem. The day has already arrived when real worshippers will worship God sincerely and honestly with the very breath of their being.

"Those are the kind of worshippers God is looking for," I explained, "because God is a spirit, and those who worship him must be sincere and respond to him from the very bottom of their hearts, and not just by going through some outward physical motions."

"Since you mentioned salvation," said the woman, "I know that a Savior is coming. They say that God will choose him and dedicate him to a very special purpose. They say that when he arrives, he will bring God's words to us and explain everything to us clearly."

"You're speaking to him," I said, "I am he."

Just then, my team returned. When they saw me talking with a woman, I could tell that they were shocked. They knew that if I had touched her, and then they touched me, they would be contaminated; but nobody interfered or asked me what I wanted from her, or why I was talking to her.

The Samaritan woman was stunned by my revelation to her. She left her water pot at the well so she could walk fast. She hurried back into town, where she found the men sitting at their usual gathering place by the city gate.

"Hey, everyone!" she said excitedly. "Quick! Hurry! There's a man sitting at Jacob's well. You have to come and see him! I just barely met him this morning. I didn't tell him anything about myself, but in the short time we spoke, he told me everything I've ever done! Couldn't he be the Savior that's supposed to be coming?"

On hearing this, the men all jumped up and rushed back to the well with her. In the meantime, my team members, who had come back from the market with food, begged me to eat a bite.

"Actually," I said, "I have food that you don't even know about!"

They wondered if maybe someone had come by and brought me something to eat while they were off shopping.

"My food is not physical food," I said. "The food that keeps me going, is to please my father who sent me down here. I live to do his will and complete his mission of saving the lost here on earth. The words from God's mouth are more essential to my survival and well-being than my necessary food.[120]

"Let me explain why. This is the time of year when you look at the fields and predict that the harvest will be ripe in just four more months or so, isn't it? I say: look up and examine the crop of people's hearts. They are already ripe and ready for the plucking!

"If you go out into the harvest of people and gather them into everlasting life, you'll be rewarded. As the prophet Daniel wrote, if you help many people turn back from their wicked ways and become friends with God again and live right, you will shine like the stars forever.[121]

"There's an old proverb that rightly says: 'One sows and another reaps; but when it's time for the harvest, both the sower and the reaper celebrate together.' I have sent you to harvest a crop on which you have not done a single day's work. Other people just like you have worked hard in the fields of humanity before you; and yet you have the privilege of joining them at the glorious end of their labors."

As I was sharing my thoughts with my team, the Samaritan woman re-appeared at the well with a large group of locals. Many of them were already convinced that I was the Savior because of the testimony of that woman, who simply said, "He told me everything I've ever done!"

They begged me to stay and spend a couple of days with them, and we did. Many more were convinced that I was the Savior because of what I shared with them during my stay.

"Now we really believe," they said to the woman after I had gone, "not because of what you told us, but because we've heard him for ourselves and we know that he really is the Savior, not just of the Hebrews, but of all the people in the world!"

26

Dangerous Fever Breaks

AFTER SPENDING THE TWO EXTRA days with the Samaritan people in Sychar, we continued on our way north. I felt God directing me back to Galilee, but I told my team that I was planning to avoid Nazareth because a prophet is never recognized in his home town.

When I arrived in Galilee, people came running out to welcome me. The men had all been at the Passover celebrations in Jerusalem.[122] Some had seen me there; others had witnessed my healing miracles and spread the word throughout the whole area and beyond, so crowds came looking for me from all over.

Since my cousin John was in prison, I was the only one left to announce the good news that everyone could now be a part of God's spiritual family! I taught in congregations throughout Galilee and the people praised and honored me everywhere I went. I just kept telling them the same story; my message was exactly the same as John's:

"God's spiritual family of believers is already being formed on earth," I kept telling people. "Look back over your lives and see if you have any regrets about the way you have behaved. Resolve to live differently and place your full confidence in God's ability to save you. Then you can be a part of God's spiritual family, because it is as close as a breath away!"

"All the things that were predicted by the prophets are supposed to happen before the Savior's mission has been completely fulfilled," I told everyone. "And they are happening all around you now!"

One day I went back to Nate's home town of Cana, where I had performed my first miracle of changing the water into wedding wine. While I was there, a wealthy nobleman who lived in Capernaum on the shores of Lake Galilee heard that I was back from Jerusalem and rushed over to see me.

"Please, I beg you, come back to Capernaum with me and heal my son! He's a grown man, but he has a terrible fever and he's in danger of dying!" he said in desperation when he found me.

"You're not willing to believe me unless you see amazing signs and spectacular miracles, are you?" I said.

"Please, Sir," he begged, "come down before he dies, and heal him!"

"Go back home," I said. "Your son has recovered. He's alive and well already!"

The man believed me. He breathed a sigh of relief and headed home. When he was almost there, some of his servants came rushing towards him, waving their arms excitedly and yelling:

"He's recovered! Your son is alive and well! He's healed! He's just fine!"

"What time did he recover?" the father asked.

"It was yesterday, Sir. His fever broke at about one o'clock in the afternoon."

The nobleman realized that this was the exact hour when I had told him that his son was well. He became a believer, and when he shared the story with his whole extended family, as well as his servants and friends, they all believed in me too.

This was the second miracle that I performed in Galilee, after I came back from the Passover festivities in Jerusalem, and I continued to travel around Galilee with my team.

27

Stunned Congregation Demands Explanation

EVENTUALLY, I DID RETURN home to Nazareth to visit my family. While there, I went to the local religious service, as I always did when I was back home. Like all Hebrew congregations, the main purpose for meeting was to study the ancient scrolls and learn about God's word. Services were held on the seventh day of each week—Saturday—which we called the Day of Rest—and I went to take part in the study.

For centuries, our people had been gathering regularly to pray and to listen to the reading of the holy scrolls which had been written by a series of men called prophets over a period of several hundred years. The prophets were inspired by God to write down what God was doing and saying in their day.

Traditionally, the women sat on one side and the men on the other, with the most important religious leaders in the front rows. At the start of the service we all recited the same blessing and made our confession of faith, called the Shema, which went like this: "Hear, O Israel, the Lord our God is the one and only God. You shall love him with all your heart, and all your soul, and all your might."[123]

Then the leader would call for any adult male to stand in front of the scrolls of holy books and pray or read a passage in Hebrew and translate it into Aramaic, our local language, so all

Stunned Congregation Demands Explanation

could understand. We didn't have bound books in those days. The holy books consisted of scrolls of paper made from a water plant called papyrus.

Then the leader would ask any competent adult male to preach a sermon. The service would end with the traditional priestly blessing originally given by Moses' brother Aaron, and repeated for centuries at the end of each gathering. It was the same blessing Uncle Zach was supposed to give the day he lost his voice.

On that particular day I was chosen to stand and read from the holy books. The men who were in charge of the scrolls brought me the one by the prophet Isaiah. I unrolled the scroll and read out loud.

"'The spirit of God is on me because he has selected me to serve him and to give the poor the good news that God has come to save humanity. He has sent me to heal the brokenhearted; to announce forgiveness for sins; to release captive sinners from their addictions, and from the grip of their sinful habits; to restore sight to the spiritually blind and to free those who are emotionally wounded. I have come to declare that this is the acceptable year chosen by God for all this to happen.'"[124]

When I finished reading, I rolled up the scroll, handed it back to the leader in charge, and sat down. Everyone's eyes were riveted to me, so I said:

"This important prediction has come true today in your presence."

"You're fantastic!" said one of the men. "We're amazed at the beauty and kindness of your words." He recognized the truth in the holy books that said I would be more wonderful than the children of men, and everything I said would be awesome and gracious.[125] But then someone asked:

"Isn't he the carpenter's son?"

"I know what you're going to say next," I said. "You'll want me to prove myself by performing miracles for you right here in Nazareth, just like the ones you've heard I did in Capernaum, like healing the nobleman's son. I know you want me to do all those great things here too! But the fact is that throughout history, no prophet has ever been accepted or respected in his own home town.

"For example, back in the prophet Elijah's day, when it failed to rain for three and a half years, the whole country was experiencing a terrible famine. There were plenty of rich Hebrew widows at the time, but God sent Elijah to a poor foreign widow's house and ordered her to feed and house him.[126]

"Later on, in the days of the prophet Elisha, there were plenty of Hebrew lepers in Israel, but God didn't heal a single one of them except Naaman, a foreign army chief from Syria!"[127]

When I said that, the people in the congregation were furious. All of a sudden I felt a firm grip on my arms. One of the toughest men there grabbed me and started pushing me out and yelling at me. Instantly, a whole mob of men joined in to push me forcibly out of the assembly hall. By the time we got outside the building, the passing crowds joined in and a spontaneous protest erupted. Instead of dropping the issue, the men of the congregation became even more determined. They dragged me violently out of town and up a hill from which you could see for thirty miles in three directions.

"Let's throw him head first over the edge of the cliffs and be

Stunned Congregation Demands Explanation

done with him!" shouted one of the religious leaders. "We don't need to listen to this! Let's splatter him on the rocks below and then he'll be quiet!"

A cheer rose up from the group as they triumphantly pulled me to the edge. But just as they were about to throw me over, I shook them off and walked away from them, unharmed. Nobody stopped me. Their initial delight had so quickly turned to violence, but when the actual moment of punishment came, I just left!

My team members were not all with me when this happened, but they soon heard about it.

"Aren't you furious with them?" they asked. "One step closer to the edge, and they could have killed you!"

"You know that God's law says it's a sin to murder anyone?" I said as we walked along. "You know it's wrong to plan to assassinate or massacre anyone with malice and forethought or out of revenge, and if you do, you'll face the death penalty?" They all nodded in agreement.[128]

"Well, I take it a step further. I believe that anger is just as wrong as murder. If you are ever angry with another human being without just cause, you should be put to death, just as if you had committed murder. In fact, if you call another person worthless or useless, you should be taken before the City Council and judged by the Hebrew Supreme Court, where even the Roman officials will uphold their decision.

"Worse yet, if you call someone an idiot, or if you scorn him by calling him stupid or moron, you should burn in the fires of hell forever, just like the garbage in the Gehenna City Dump where the trash is burned.

"Don't you remember how King David's wife, Queen Michal, had contempt for her husband and ridiculed him to his face? She even mocked him in public. As a result, King David sent her out of his life. She lost her position as queen, and was never able to have a child with him.[129]

"Living in peace and getting along with other people is of the utmost importance. So important, in fact, that if you ever bring your offering for the support of the temple to the altar, and then suddenly remember that someone has something against you, don't be a hypocrite. Leave your gift at the altar and don't even think of offering it to God. Instead, go find that person and get reconciled, regardless of who is at fault. Then go back to the altar and offer your gift to God.

"Anger is so destructive that I don't ever want you to rush into a quarrel or complaint with anyone. You just never know how it will turn out. You have no idea what your opponent will say about you, and you might not be able to wiggle out of an embarrassing situation.[130] Starting a quarrel is like bursting a dam, so it's better to calm yourself down and make the smart choice of giving up your position before it can be challenged.

"If you are already in a quarrel and it has escalated to involve lawyers, do everything you can to settle the issue out of court, even if you have to make a deal with your accuser at the last minute on the courthouse steps. Because if you don't, he could have you arrested and drag you before the judge. The judge could turn you over to the officer and have you thrown in jail! At that point, I promise you that you won't get out till you've paid your fine to the last penny, or completed your whole sentence.

Stunned Congregation Demands Explanation

"Instead of rushing into a heated argument when you are angry, run to God while he may be found,[131] because if you wait till 'someday' to turn to him, it could be too late![132]

The cliff-top incident left us all deep in thought. The prophet was right. I could do nothing in my hometown of Nazareth. I decided to move to Capernaum, a peaceful town on the shores of Lake Galilee important enough to house a Roman tax office. One of Governor Herod's chief officers lived there and he had built a lovely new religious meeting hall for our people, where I could go to the weekly services.

I went to Capernaum to fulfill the prediction of the prophet Isaiah who wrote that the people in the area of Lake Galilee, called Zebulun and Naphtali, who lived in darkness and ignorance, would one day see a great Light.[133]

This Light would shine on those who were always in fear of some kind of disaster and those experiencing the heartache and loneliness of a life without God. This Light would open the eyes of the blind and swing wide the prison doors of the emotionally trapped. This Light would rescue those who were living in ignorance and free them from the dark prison cells of their own self-centeredness.[134]

My goal was to announce to everyone that God's spiritual community on earth was already springing into existence.

"Clean up your lives," I kept telling everyone. "Ask for forgiveness and change your life. Then you'll be able to draw close to God. I'm telling you that it's possible to pray and have intimacy with God, but only when you are ready to let go of your past and your evil habits, and willing to obey him and follow his ways."

28

A Classroom With A View

ONE DAY I WAS WALKING along the shores of Lake Galilee when I spotted Peter and Andrew out in their boats, fishing. They had their own fishing business and when they weren't with me, they were out making a living with their nets. Sometimes they sailed out onto the lake; at other times they fished from the shore. Often they would wade into the water up to their chests and throw the nets out in front of them in the shape of a ring. The nets would sink below the surface like conical traps.

That day they were out on the lake with all kinds of casting nets and I watched as they took the nets and arranged them on their arms, ready to toss them in the water. They also had sweeping nets and dragnets with floats which they pulled along behind their boats when in deeper waters.

"Hey, guys!" I called out to them. "Come and work full-time with me and I'll turn you into fishermen who literally fish for lost people swimming aimlessly in the sea of life!"

"All right, then." they said. The two brothers pulled into shore, put up all their equipment, and came with me without hesitation.

We walked a little farther and saw James and John, their fishing partners. They were sitting in their family boat with their father Zebedee and their employees, quietly mending their nets and watching what was going on. Their mother, Salome, was home cooking.

"James! John!" I called out to them. "Come follow me in full-time service!" The two brothers pulled into shore, got out of their boat and joined me right away, leaving their father and his employees to run the business without them. Zebedee would have quite a story to tell their mother that night!

A few days later, I was teaching my team mates on a three-mile stretch of lakeside farmland called Gennesaret, which means Garden of Riches. It was a beautiful fertile area, with groves of figs, olives, palms and walnut trees all along the shore. A crowd gathered, eager to hear my words and become my followers, and it wasn't long before I was completely surrounded by masses of people and couldn't even move.

Our custom was for the teacher to teach from a sitting position and the listeners to remain standing, out of respect; but if I did that, the people wouldn't be able to see me. As I looked around for a more practical place from which to speak, I noticed that there were two empty boats by the shore. Some fishermen had already climbed out and were rinsing off all the various kinds of nets.

"One of those boats is mine," said Peter, who had been out fishing all night. "You can borrow it if you like."

"Great! Go ahead and push out a little from the shore," I said as I climbed into the boat with Peter. I sat down and began to teach the people directly from the boat. They stood around respectfully and listened to what I had to say.

"As humans, you are not perfect." I explained. "In fact, your natural behavior is often the exact opposite of God's way. God has always known that. He sees how wicked you are, and how you fantasize about doing bad things, even in your youth.[135]

"But there is something you have in common with God: you love your kids! No matter how flawed and sinful you may be, you would do anything for your kids, wouldn't you? If your son asked you for bread, would you give him a plate with a rock on it? Of course not! Or if your daughter asked you for some fish, would you hand her a snake? Of course not! Or if your toddler asked you for some eggs, would you serve him a scorpion? Of course not!

"If you, imperfect as you are, love your kids and know instinctively how to give them good things, don't you know that God, who is your perfect heavenly father, is so much more eager to give you good things if you ask him? And those good gifts include his holy Spirit—his presence in your life on a daily basis!

"Remember that God has creative new plans and purposes for you. His plans are not evil or second rate, but plans for peace; plans that will give you hope that you can have the beautiful life that you dream of; plans that will give you something to live for!"[136]

"But remember that while you're asking God to give you good things for yourself, and while you're waiting for the good that you want others to do for you, you still need to treat others just like you would want them to treat you. In fact, if I were to summarize the whole point of God's law and all the words of God's prophets, I would give you one simple statement: Treat people exactly the way you would like them to treat you. That's because God declared from the beginning that you must 'love your neighbor as yourself.'"[137]

A Classroom With A View

When I finished teaching, the happy crowd wandered off.

"Now let's push away from the shore, Peter," I said. "I want you to go where the water is really deep and let down your nets."

"Sir," said Peter, "we fished all through the night and we didn't catch a thing! But if you want me to go out into deeper waters and let down the nets, let's go!"

Peter and I sailed away from the shore and dropped a dragnet into the water. To Peter's surprise, we soon pulled in a huge catch of fish, to the point that the net was starting to tear!

"Hey, guys! Come over here!" we yelled to some fishermen in another boat. Waving wildly, we signaled that we needed help. They rowed over as quickly as they could and helped us pull the loaded net up into the boat. We ended up catching so many fish that we filled both the boats until they looked like they were going to sink.

When Peter saw how huge the catch was, he sensed that he was in the presence of something supernatural. He fell down at my knees.

"Oh, Sir…" he exclaimed. "I see that you're a miracle worker! I don't even dare approach you. I'm not good enough; I don't deserve to be with you! I'm just a sinful man, and you have given me this incredible catch of fish!"

"Don't be afraid of me, Peter," I said. "From now on, you'll catch men in the same way you caught all these fish—by going fishing when and where I tell you!"

Everyone who was involved in helping us pull in the catch, including Peter's partners, James and John, were amazed at the huge number of fish we had caught. When we got back to the shore, the rest of the fishermen who had helped us pull in the huge catch simply walked away from everything they owned and became part of my team. They too, were ready to go with me wherever I went.

29

Crazy Man Disrupts Religious Service

WE RETURNED TO THE HOUSE in Capernaum and I spent a lot of time getting my team members ready and teaching them privately. On the Day of Rest we would all go together to the local religious service. At one meeting, I was again asked to comment on a passage in the scrolls.

"Let's talk about keeping our commitments," I said. "Do we always have to keep our word no matter the circumstances? You know that God doesn't want you to make rash promises to each other, or vow to do something you will later regret.

"You make promises to each other in everyday life, as well as in legal and state affairs and important ceremonies. Unfortunately, you think that if you take a complicated, formal-sounding oath, it is binding; but if you just say you will do something, you can easily change your mind and get out of it!

"But I say that you should always be honest and transparent and say what you mean. The holy books teach us that we should keep our word—and simply do what we say we will do![138]

"So I say, don't make promises to God, because if you do, you will have to keep them.[139] And don't ever swear; not by heaven, because it's God's throne; nor by earth, because it's God's footstool. Don't even swear by your own head, because you can't change your hair from one color to another just by speaking!

"Don't tell people what they want to hear, just to be polite. Instead, communicate clearly. Simply say what you mean, and mean what you say! If someone asks you to do something or to agree to something, simply say 'Yes' or 'No'. Anything more involved or elaborate than that just complicates things and has evil intent."

"Sir, you teach in a way that really helps us understand the holy books. It's amazing!" they said. "You're totally unlike our professors, who are supposedly the legal experts on religious matters. You're different! You speak with confidence and authority, and there's power in your words!"

Many in the congregation nodded their agreement, but one of them got up.

"Get away from us, Jesus of Nazareth!" he screamed out suddenly. Shaking his fist at me, he yelled: "Leave us alone! We don't want you near us! Have you come to destroy us? I know who you are! You're the Holy One of God!"

"Stop talking and come out of him right now!" I ordered the demon inside the man. Instantly, the man began to shake. The evil spirit threw him to the ground and came out of him with a blood-curdling scream.

Everyone was startled and rushed to help the man to his feet. Much to their surprise, he was completely unhurt by the fall. He was calm and smiling and everyone could see that he was fine. But the incident had shocked and frightened the congregation and they wondered what on earth was going on.

"What a powerful teacher!" I heard them say to one another in awe. "He must have a higher level of understanding of the holy books than we do, to be able to do this! It's impressive to watch him order the evil spirits around! He has such a commanding presence and so much power and conviction in his voice that even demons obey his command!"

30

Patients Line Up For Free Health Care

PETER AND ANDREW INVITED ME back to their house after the service, together with James and John. Peter's wife met us at the door, panic written all over her face.

"What's wrong, Dear?" Peter asked.

"It's Mamma! She's really sick!"

"What seems to be the problem?" I asked.

"Come look!" she said in desperation. "She's burning up! I've tried everything, but I can't get her fever down. Can you heal her?"

I went to her mother's side and stood over her. Taking her hand in mine, I said:

"Fever leave!" The instant I touched her hand, her fever broke.

"Let me help you get up out of bed," I volunteered.

"Thank you," she said, smiling, "but I suddenly feel just fine! Let me get dressed and I'll make you a nice, home-cooked meal!"

Sure enough, it wasn't long before she emerged and started to busy herself in the kitchen, serving us her delicious home-made food.

Meanwhile, word of the possessed man's deliverance in the middle of the service spread like wildfire throughout the whole region of Galilee and that very evening, as the sun began to set, people started to show up at Peter's house. They brought every kind of sick and possessed person to me for healing. Before long, it looked like the whole town was gathered outside the door.

I went out and touched each of them, healing them from every kind of disease. I was fulfilling the prophet Isaiah's words, when he wrote that I would take people's sickness on myself and carry their grief and sorrow.[140]

I also threw out many evil spirits by demanding them to come out of the people. Many of the demons yelled, "You're the Son of God!" as they came out. I ordered them to be silent and I didn't allow them to say a word, because they knew who I was, and I didn't want them advertising it. Only the Roman Emperor Augustus Caesar had called himself the Son of God. Anyone else claiming a similar title would be crucified.

When everyone was healed and taken care of, they finally left and we spent the night with Peter and his family. I didn't sleep long. Instead, I got up several hours before daybreak and slipped quietly out of the house to pray. I wanted to be alone, so I walked off into the night to a solitary place where I could spend time in prayer, undisturbed.

When Peter and the other three woke up and discovered that I was gone, they went to look for me.

"Everyone's searching for you!" they said, when they eventually found me. "They all want you!" But I refused to go back to the house.

"Let's move on," I said. "We need to go to other towns so that I can tell more people the good news and let them know that God's spiritual family is already in existence and available to them. That is my mission!"

Several of my team members tried to grab me and physically stop me from leaving.

"Let me go!" I said. "I want to travel throughout Galilee and teach in all the congregations here. I plan to let everyone know that a personal relationship with God is possible!"

So we kept on walking from town to town. Everywhere we went, I healed people of all kinds of diseases and problems, and I cast out demon spirits. Word of my miraculous healings spread all the way across the border to Syria, and people came from far and wide to ask for my help. They brought many who had serious physical conditions, including paralysis and epilepsy.

They also brought many who were in mental anguish and psychological torment. Some were suffering from mental illness, while others were demon-possessed. I healed them all, no matter the cause or the severity of their suffering.

Huge crowds continued to pursue me because of my miracles. Whenever I spoke before a congregation, people came to hear me from all over Galilee. Some came all the way from Jerusalem and every part of Judea. Others even came from beyond the Jordan River, carrying their loved ones, desperate for my help. They were not disappointed, because I healed them all.

Hearing that I was going to be in town, one of the people who came looking for my help was a man covered with leprosy. Lepers were outcasts and had to live outside the city because they were considered highly contagious. This one had been determined enough to break through the social barriers and seek me out. When he reached me, he fell to his knees adoringly, and begged for my help.

"Sir, I know that if you want to, you can make my leprosy go away!"

I was really moved by this man's trust. I reached out and touched him.

"Of course I want you to be healthy and live a normal life!" I said. "Be healed!" The instant I spoke, the man's leprosy vanished and he was clear of all symptoms. Then I gave him a strict warning:

"Don't breathe a word of this to anyone, but first go and show yourself to the priest, like you're supposed to. The holy books say that the priest has to go outside the city to where the dead are buried and where you lepers live, and he has to examine you if you claim to be healed. The priest is trained to carefully look at every inch of your skin before certifying that you are completely symptom-free.

"If you are certified as healed, then you have to make the purification sacrifice for healed lepers as Moses commanded. You must gather two birds, two perfect lambs, cedar wood, scarlet dye, sweet-smelling Egyptian mint, fine flour, and oil. You have to take all those to the priest and offer the purification sacrifice before you can be admitted back into the city and back into society."[141]

My warning didn't seem to make any difference to the healed leper! He was so excited that he couldn't contain his joy. Instead of keeping quiet and going to the priest, he rushed off and shared his good news with anyone and everyone who would listen.

"I'm healed!" he kept saying, looking down at his new body. "You can hug me now! I can hug you now! I can have friends now!

I can move back into town again! Glory to God! I am miraculously healed!" Crowds gathered as he broadcasted it everywhere. He gave such a detailed report that dozens more came to me to be healed.

From then on, it was impossible for me to come and go as I pleased. I hadn't planned to be a celebrity, but everywhere I went, people recognized me and chased after me. I couldn't stay in Capernaum anymore because we never had any privacy. I took my team to deserted areas in the countryside so we could pray; but even so, people still managed to track me down and come from all over to ask for my help.

31

Four Men Break Into Private Home

WE CONTINUED TO CRISS-CROSS Galilee with the good news on foot and by boat. Since the area was on an important trade route between Egypt and the Far East, new ideas and products were free to flow through the region. The market-places in the towns and villages buzzed with exciting new conversations. Herod's new capital of Tiberias was booming and the olive oil export business was thriving.

The population of Galilee was very diverse, with many people of foreign descent dating back to the Assyrian conquest. They all spoke with a very pronounced local Aramaic accent different from that of the more conservative south around Jerusalem.

After teaching for weeks all over Galilee, I was ready to go back to Peter's house in Capernaum. We tried to sneak back into town by boat, but it didn't work! As soon as people saw that I was back, word spread and immediately they began to flock to the house again. Many scholars and Spiritual Ones came from every village in Galilee and Judea, and even from Jerusalem, to listen to me. They brought many who were sick, and the healing power of God was in me to heal them all.

It was clear that the people were hungry for my words. Day after day, I taught them about God. Strangers from far and wide crowded into Peter's house until it was packed so tightly that nobody could even squeeze in past the front door!

"Let me tell you what your life needs to be like for you to be a true believer," I taught them. "If you come to me and listen carefully to what I have to say, and then you actually put my words into practice, you're like a wise man who built his house on a rock.

"Here's how he went about it: first, he dug a deep hole all the way down to the bed rock and then he pulled out a huge amount of soil. He spent a lot of money on equipment and transportation to carry all that soil out of the way. Then, when the earth was completely cleared away, he was able to lay a solid foundation directly on the rock surface and start building his dream home. He was a very thorough and practical man. He did the job right, without compromise.

"One day, not long after he had finished building, it started to drizzle, and then to rain hard. The rain poured down, flooding the surrounding area. There was so much water that the rivers swelled and the floodwaters rose. The winds reached gale force speeds, beating against the house. The rivers burst their banks and overflowed into the surrounding neighborhoods.

"Then a wall of water rushed like a tsunami towards the wise man's house, but the house held up just fine. It didn't capsize like the other houses around him. No matter how hard the wind and the waves battered that house, it couldn't be shaken because its foundation was built on solid rock.

"On the other hand, if you listen to my teachings but you don't put them into practice in your everyday life, it proves that you are not a believer. Don't fool yourself! You're like a foolish man who built his dream home on sandy soil, without ever putting down a solid foundation.

"When the winds beat against this man's house, it collapsed immediately. When the rains came, the floodwaters smashed into the walls and rushed into the house, submerging everything in sight. The house collapsed and the walls fell apart with a loud noise. Pieces of his dream home were scattered far and wide, never to be recovered!

"If you build your life on my teachings by putting them into practice in your everyday life, then, when problems and difficulties come, they won't be able to touch you. But if you just listen to me, without actually doing what I tell you to do, then when life's problems and difficulties hit you, you'll collapse, just like the house that was built on sand. You'll feel like you have crashed and fallen apart, and the pieces of your life will be scattered far and wide, never to be recovered."

As I was teaching, four men showed up outside Peter's house, carrying a weak, paralyzed friend on a stretcher. They had tried desperately to get in to see me, but the crowds at the doors and windows were packed so tightly that even though they yelled and banged on the doors, nobody would let them through.

"We can't give up now!" one of them said. "I have an idea!" The four men climbed up onto the flat roof that was designed to catch rainwater for bathing. Then they hoisted the handicapped man on the stretcher up onto the roof. As soon as they figured out what room I was in, they quickly poked a hole in the roof and cut a large opening through the ceiling above me. Once the hole was big enough, they carefully lowered the man down on the stretcher, right in front of me, which caused quite a stir.

When I saw how determined they were to get their paralyzed friend into the house to see me, and how totally confident they were that I would heal him, I stopped teaching and spoke to the sick man.

"Cheer up, Son, your sins are forgiven," I said.

"How can he say something so outrageous?" the religious professors and Spiritual Ones in the crowd wondered out loud. "He says he's forgiving the man's sins! That's something only God can do! This man is insulting God! Only God can bring a clean thing out of an unclean and immoral one.[142] Only God can blot out our intentional deviation and our premeditated sin. Only God can forgive and forget."[143]

I knew what they were thinking. I could tell that they were trying to use their natural reason to rationalize what was going on, or to discredit me. They knew God to be the only one who can forgive sins, so they were struggling with my words.

"Why are you thinking wicked thoughts and trying to figure this out with your minds?" I asked. "What do you think is easier to do? Tell the paralyzed man that his sins are forgiven, or say, 'Get up, pick up your stretcher and go home?' But just so you know that I do have God's authority and permission to dismiss sins on earth, here's what I have to say to this man: 'Get up, friend. Roll up your stretcher and go home!'"

To everyone's surprise, the paralyzed man got up. The people in the room stepped back as he walked around before our very eyes. Then he bent over, rolled up his stretcher and carried it out into the street, where he paraded around and showed everyone how well he could walk. Then he did exactly what I had told him. He took his stretcher and headed home!

"We've never seen anything like this before!" the people said in amazement! Many of them were awestruck and afraid, recognizing the invisible power of God. "We had no idea that God could give such power to men!" they exclaimed. They couldn't understand that I was completely one with God, which is precisely why I was able to forgive the man's sins and send him on his way healed!

32

Holy Man Spotted On Bad Side Of Town

ON ANOTHER OCCASION I WAS walking along the shore of Lake Galilee when someone recognized me, and immediately, a crowd of people, hungry to hear about God, gathered around me.

"Today I'm going to explain a spiritual concept by using a natural comparison," I said. "God's spiritual family grows unnoticeably. Picture an insignificant little mustard seed. One day you plant the tiny seed into the ground; when you come back, you are amazed to find that it has grown into a tree twice as tall as a man! It is now home to all kinds of birds that fly around in the sky and come to it for shade and a safe place to build their nests. You never actually see the mustard seed as it is being transformed into a tree!

"Let me give you another example. God's influence is invisible, like yeast, which is used to make bread rise. A woman takes the yeast and hides it in just the right amount of dough. Then she leaves the dough alone. Meanwhile, the ball of dough rises and puffs up into a loaf of bread.

"The prophet Isaiah explained that even though God's spiritual family starts small, it eventually spreads to all the nations of the world!"[144]

After I had finished teaching, I walked along the waterfront and passed by a busy customs booth. A Hebrew tax collector was collecting taxes for the Roman conquerors. Our people generally hated these men, considering them to be traitors because they collaborated with the occupying Romans. Most of them were corrupt. They forced our people to pay bribes which were supposedly for the Roman officials, but many of them lined their own pockets with a portion of the money they collected.

As I looked over at the booth, I saw the tax collector sitting at his desk, cashiering and I went over to talk to him. As we chatted, I learned that his name was Matthew.

"Come with me, Matthew," I said. "I want you to travel with me full-time and be on my team."

Matthew had heard all about me. He was so excited that he immediately got up from his desk, locked up his booth, and walked away from his job to follow me. Out of gratitude, he decided to throw a big party for me at his home. He invited all his tax collector friends, as well as some known criminals. He prepared a delicious meal and invited my whole team, which by this time had grown to quite a few people, to come and sit down with him and enjoy the food.

Of course, the respectable religious teachers and the Spiritual Ones soon heard about the party and came by to check things out. When they saw me sitting and eating with corrupt and dishonest men, they were disgusted and complained to my team members behind my back.

"Why are you and the teacher sitting down to eat with traitors and scoundrels like these?" they asked. "Don't you know that sharing a meal with someone signals to others that you agree with their lifestyle?"

I found out what they were saying.

"People who are strong and in good health," I explained, "don't need to see a doctor; but those who are sick do. I haven't come to call people who are already living by God's standards. No. I've come to call those who keep falling short of his requirements. I want them to take a good look at themselves, learn from their mistakes and change their ways!

"You should go and read the words of the prophet Hosea. He wrote that God prefers mercy over sacrifice. God wants people to act with compassion towards their fellow man, rather than proudly offer religious sacrifices to him.[145]

"I haven't come to call the good people who already want to meet God's expectations. No. I've come to call those who are far from God and who keep messing up over and over. I want them to look back at their actions and reflect on their past. I want them to realize what they're doing wrong and change their lifestyles."

33

Secrets to Successful Fasting

ONE DAY, SOME OF MY cousin John's followers came to me with a question about fasting, which was a common religious practice in my day.

"Our teacher, John, says we should spend a lot of time in prayer and fasting for religious reasons," they said, "and so do the Spiritual Ones. So why do your team members go around eating and drinking and enjoying themselves?"

"If you were at a wedding," I explained, "would you expect the wedding party to fast and mourn during the reception, while the bride and groom are enjoying the cake? Of course not! So long as the groom is celebrating, they wouldn't dream of fasting. But once the celebration is over and the groom leaves, then they are free to fast. Now my friends are celebrating while I'm with them. Later, they'll have plenty of time to fast when I'm gone."

They stood there, looking at me, obviously not convinced, so I decided to give them some more illustrations to make my point.

"If you had a hole in your favorite item of clothing, would you patch the hole with a brand new piece of cloth that had never been washed? Of course not! Because when you go to wash the garment, the new cloth would shrink and rip the old cloth away, making the hole much worse than it was to begin with!

"By the same token, if you had an old wineskin which was already stretched to the maximum, would you take fresh, unfermented wine and pour it in? Of course not! Because the new wine would start to ferment and the already over-stretched wineskin would burst. The wine would splatter all over the place and the wineskin would be torn beyond repair. You have to pour freshly squeezed grape juice into brand new wine skins that will stretch to accommodate the fermentation of the wine!

"If you were enjoying a drink of fine aged wine, would you want a refill of fresh, unfermented wine? Of course not! Because you know that the mature wine tastes so much better, and you'd want to drink that instead of a cheap substitute.

"My team members understand that I am with them right now. That's why they are really enjoying being with me while I'm here, instead of fasting, which they will be free to do once I'm gone!"

"Fasting does have its benefits," I said. "But if you want to enjoy those benefits, don't be like the hypocrites who like to impress everyone with their religious lifestyle. They want to make sure people know they are fasting by putting ashes on their faces. They walk around looking weak and tired, with messy hair and wrinkled clothing. Then they really stand out in a crowd and everyone can tell that they are fasting.

"Guess what? They get their full reward right there and then, when people see them and admire them for being spiritual. But that is all the attention they'll ever get because God is not impressed.

"Don't be like them. Instead, when you fast, take a shower; put on clean clothes and wash your face so you can look fresh and clean and normal. That way, nobody will have a clue that you're fasting. Don't worry. God will see what you're doing in secret and he'll reward you publicly.

"Make sure your fasting doesn't lead you to become self-absorbed. If it does, it's time to look at it differently. Do you really want to spend your time beating yourself up with guilt, and hanging your head in shame and crying pitifully? Is this what you call a fast that is pleasing and acceptable to God? [146] Am I saying that you should not fast? Of course not!

"God himself understands what true fasting is about. He says that if you really want to fast, then take your focus off yourself. Instead, set people free from the grasp of their evil habits and problem situations. Lift the heavy burdens off their backs. Release the downtrodden from being exploited. Fight to bring an end to every type of slavery. Distribute your food to the hungry. Welcome the poor and homeless into your homes and clothe those who are naked or in rags.

"Don't hide from the needs of your own family members. Offer your time and concern to people who are lonely and struggling with their problems. Remove all injustice from your environment. Stop pointing your finger and criticizing others, and stop wasting time talking about superficial and sinful matters.[147]

"If you do all these things, God will reward you greatly. Life and happiness will burst into your life like the rays of the morning sun. Your physical and emotional well-being will bounce quickly back to a state of complete health. You'll always know the right thing to do. You'll enjoy the glory, majesty and wealth of God's presence and blessings in your life. Whenever you call on him, he'll answer you. Whenever you cry out to him, he'll say, 'Here I am.'"

34

Pool Man Walks After 38 Years

I CONTINUED GOING UP TO Jerusalem with all the other Hebrew men for the major religious holidays throughout the year. On one of those trips, I took advantage of the Day of Rest to take a walk along the city wall near the Sheep Gate.

As I walked along, I remembered how, centuries earlier, God had allowed the north to be conquered by the Assyrians, and later, the south, including Jerusalem, to be conquered by the Babylonians. This all happened because of the people's continuous disobedience. In the attack on Jerusalem, the city walls had collapsed and the beautiful temple built by King David's son, Solomon, was destroyed.

The fall of Jerusalem came as a total shock to our ancestors, who thought they were immune from punishment, just because they were the children of God. Many of them were carried off to Babylon, about fifty miles south of Baghdad in Iraq. Once they got there, they were shocked by what they saw. Babylon was the world capital of paganism, with over fifty temples dedicated to pagan gods.

The exile to Babylon was the saddest period of our people's history. They were put to work as slaves, building canals, waterways, beautifully manicured parks and impressive buildings for King Nebuchadnezzar, who wanted to make his city the grandest in the world. Already, the Babylonians were proud of their famous hanging gardens, which were one of the seven wonders of the ancient world, and they happily used our ancestors to make their city even more famous.

Eventually, the Hebrews started to trickle back to Jerusalem. The prophet Nehemiah, a great Hebrew leader, took a group and organized the rebuilding of the city walls. Under his direction, they built a gate in the walls and called it Sheep Gate.[148]

Close to Sheep Gate was a spring-fed pool called Bethesda, which means house of grace. It was surrounded by five covered porches. A lot of blind, crippled and chronically ill people used to lie in the shady colonnades by the pool, waiting for their miracle. They believed that an angel would come down into the pool at unexpected times known only to God and make the water tremble. Whoever managed to get into the pool first, when the water started to tremble, would be totally healed.

Lying on a mat near Sheep Gate was a man who had been sick for thirty-eight years. When I saw him I knew he had been a cripple for a very long time.

"Do you really want to be healed?" I asked him.

"My relatives have been dropping me off here every morning for years," the powerless man complained bitterly. "But once they leave, I don't have anyone to grab me and carry me into the pool whenever the water trembles, so I try to make it by myself; but whenever I start to get up and walk, some other lucky person always manages to get into the water ahead of me!" The man clearly was full of excuses to justify his predicament.

"Get up right now!" I ordered the man. "You don't need the pool water. Just pick up your mat and start walking!"

Shocked, the man got up, picked up his mat and started walking normally. His healing caused quite a sensation, because it happened on the Day of Rest. It wasn't long before people cornered him and accused him of breaking the law.

"Today is the Day of Rest!" they said. "It's a religious holiday and you know you're not allowed to do any kind of work, such as carrying your mat!" they declared. Technically, they were right. God's law required that nobody—not even a slave or an animal—was to do any kind of work on the Day of Rest.[149]

People were not allowed to lift anything—or to carry any burden or package on the Day of Rest—not even on the back of a pack animal. They couldn't carry anything through the city gates. All commerce had to stop by sundown on Friday night. All carts carrying fresh fruits and vegetables had to be inside the city before dark.[150] Nobody was allowed to do any skilled labor, crafts, ministry, service, errands, everyday business, or even royal business commanded by the king.

The people were in a panic, because they believed that the healed man's actions would bring great distress to the city. According to the holy books, the consequences of working on the Day of Rest were very serious. If anyone disobeyed, even if they just picked up a package and carried it through the city gates of Jerusalem, God would light a wild fire in the gate that would burn down the city with its palaces and beautiful homes, just like when the Babylonians invaded.[151]

Ever since God had delivered them from slavery in Egypt and brought them to the Promised Land, the Hebrews had believed they were safe forever. So when the Babylonians invaded and carried them off into slavery in Babylon, they couldn't believe it was happening! Now, they were determined never to go back into slavery again. If they saw anyone working on the Day of Rest, everyone over-reacted, thinking some terrible disaster might happen again.

If, on the other hand, the people obeyed and rested one day out of seven, Jerusalem would be blessed with great leaders. Descendants of the wonderful King David would continue to sit on the throne in Jerusalem. The city would last for eternity, and other nations would come from around the world to worship God there.[152]

"It's not my fault!" explained the man who was now perfectly healed. "Carrying the mat wasn't my idea. I've been lying here sick, minding my own business for thirty-eight years, but today a man came along and healed me completely, once and for all! He's the one who told me to pick up my mat and carry it off with me!"

"Who are you talking about?" they asked.

"I have no idea who he is!" the man replied. "He healed me and told me to pick up my mat and start walking. I bent over to pick up my mat, and when I looked up, he was gone!"

Later that day, I made a point of finding the man. He was in the temple, thanking God for his healing.

"Look, man," I said to him. "You're completely well now. Stop being such a complainer. If you go back to your bad habits and negative thoughts, and start whining and complaining again, you'll go back to being sick and end up in worse shape than before!"

The man was stunned and didn't say a word. He knew exactly what I was talking about. He left the temple and went to tell the leaders that I was the one who had healed him. When they realized it was me, they planned to catch me and punish me. I had really made them angry because I had healed the man on the Day of Rest.

35

Mirror Images

"SOME PEOPLE ARE FURIOUS with me for what I'm doing," I explained to my team members, "but I can't do anything by myself. I can only do what I see God, my father, doing. Whatever he does, I do too. He and I are mirror images of each other. He loves me and he loves to demonstrate everything he's doing to me. He'll show me how to do even greater miracles than these in order for you to be amazed at his power."

It wasn't long before crowds began to gather as usual.

"God sees you all as equal," I explained. "In fact, he doesn't even judge you. Instead, he has committed the power of sentencing people to life or death to me, because he wants everyone to honor and respect me, just like they honor and respect him. If you don't honor me, you don't honor God who sent me!" Some of them looked shocked.

"If you listen to my words and commit your life to God, you already have constant and never-ending spiritual life," I promised. "You will not have to stand before God at the Last Judgment, because you have already moved beyond sentencing and on to everlasting life.

"Remember the vision where the prophet Daniel saw someone who looked like the 'Son of Man' coming before God in the clouds?" I asked them. Everyone nodded. "Well, God gave the

Son of Man full control over everything, so that all people would serve him forever.[153] I am that Son of Man.

"Even though I came from heaven, I am just as human as you are," I said, holding out my arms so they could see my physical body. "That means that I am fully qualified to judge you, because I know what it is like to be human," I explained, looking at each one of them with deep love. "But when I judge you, I do it based only on what I hear in heaven. This means that I'm always fair with everyone, because I'm committed to doing the will of God who sent me here.

"God is so powerful," I said, "that he can bring dead people back to life—and so can I! God is brimming over with vibrant life—and so am I! God has been working miracles since eternity began—and so have I!"

The group listened to me, mesmerized.

"Soon, even the dead will hear my voice and come back to life!" I continued. "I don't want you to be shocked, but one day all those who are dead and buried will hear my voice and come out of their graves. Corpses will rise from the dust of their graves and come back to life!"[154]

"Remember how the prophet Daniel predicted that many who sleep in the dust of the earth would awake, some to everlasting life, and some to shame and suffering?" I asked. Everyone nodded.[155] "Those who have lived useful and profitable lives will live happily forever. Those who have been evil and done wicked things will be punished at the Last Judgment.

"Those of you who are educated might be listening to me and thinking: 'Wait a minute! Even in a lawsuit, you have to have at least two or three eye-witnesses to give testimony to establish a fact.[156] So where are the witnesses to testify that this man is telling the truth?'

"Let me answer that. First, there's John the Baptist, who burned as gloriously as a brightly shining lamp, even when nobody was looking. For a while, you were glad to jump for joy in front of his ever-burning flame, and listen when he clearly told you who I am. But you have already forgotten what John said. You don't know how to be faithful to God because there is no light in you.[157]

"Second, there are the miracles I have done. They are more powerful testimony than any words a man could give. My actions are proof that God is my father and that he endorses me through the miracles that I'm performing! If you knew God, you would recognize God in me. But you don't believe me because you've never heard God's voice, nor seen what he looks like.

"Third, there are the prophets. Go ahead, read where they predicted over and over that the Lord will raise up a prophet who speaks God's words and not his own. 'God will put his words in the prophet's mouth and he will tell the people all that God commands.'[158] That is what is happening before your eyes! But you don't recognize it because there is no light in you and you don't know how to follow God.[159]

"I'm telling you all these things so that you can be saved from God's anger against sin! Not because I need your help to endorse me. But I know that you don't really care, because you don't really love God! Do you know how I know that?"

Nobody said a word. They were shocked.

"I know you don't love God because you haven't welcomed me, even though I come from God," I said.

"If someone else came on his own, you'd welcome him, wouldn't you?" I asked. "Or if your friend's son came to visit, you would welcome him for your friend's sake! Why is it that you so easily believe what other people say, but you don't believe the most priceless words I bring you directly from God?" I looked around at their stubborn faces. Everyone was silent, listening. I could tell that the religious leaders were furious.

"Don't think that I will accuse you to God," I said sternly. "There is someone else who will accuse you—and that someone is Moses, whom you say you trust. If you really trusted Moses, you would recognize who I am. If you really believed Moses, you would believe me, because he wrote about me. But you obviously don't believe what he wrote, and you don't believe me either!"

The religious leaders took off in a huff, determined to kill me. They were furious with me for two reasons. First, in their opinion, I had violated the Day of Rest by having the man carry his mat on a day when working or carrying things was forbidden.

Second, I had called God my father. That was too shocking for them. They agreed that I had insulted God and was guilty of the religious crime of blasphemy by saying that I was equal to God. They wanted to kill me since I had done these two things on a holy day, because that's what the law prescribed for these sins.

36

Looking Good In Public

ON ANOTHER DAY OF REST I was walking along with my team in the countryside when the Spiritual Ones got upset with us again. They noticed that as we were walking through a field, my team members were plucking grains of wheat, rolling them around in their fingertips and eating them because they were hungry.

The holy books didn't allow us to do the work of harvesting on the Day of Rest,[160] but they did allow us to pick grain by hand and nibble it when walking through a neighbor's field. The Spiritual Ones were so legalistic that they objected even to what was allowed.

"Look at your people!" they protested. "Don't they know that they're not supposed to do any work on the Day of Rest? Don't they know about our nation's punishment in the Babylonian exile? Don't they realize they are putting all the rest of us in danger of another national disaster?"

I knew they were wrong.

"Have you ever read what King David did?" I asked them. "You remember when he and his men were starving? They went into God's house and asked the high priest for food; and he gave them some holy bread because that's all he had?[161] Technically, only the priests could eat the bread after it had been offered to God.[162] Nobody else was allowed to eat it, not even a king. Yet the priest gave it to David, and he ate some and shared the rest with his men.

"The whole point of that story is that people are more important than things! People were not created for food, but food was created for people! In the same way, people were not created for the Day of Rest, but the Day of Rest was created for people. God's design for you is to have one day a week off from daily duties so you can spend it being thankful for all the good things he has done for you.

"Do you remember the very first permanent temple building built by King David's son, Solomon? King Solomon said that not even the heavens could contain God, much less a temple building!ature[163]

"Well, today there is someone in the sacred temple who is more sacred than the building itself. Remember that the prophet Malachi predicted that the Lord would suddenly come to his temple?[164] I am here now, and being with me is more important than the restrictions of the Day of Rest. I am greater than the Day of Rest!

"The holy books say that if you had to choose between being merciful to people, and offering religious sacrifices to God—then being merciful is more important. If you had to choose between knowing God and offering him lots of burnt offerings—the relationship with God is more important.[165]

"Do you think God really wants you to present yourself before him with thousands of sacrificial rams and rivers of oil, or give your first-born son to pay for your sins? Of course not!

Looking Good In Public

"God wants you to be fair and just with others; to love passionately; to forgive generously; to help those in need and to walk humbly with him.[166] God is interested in how you treat him and others. He doesn't put things above relationships. If you understood this, you wouldn't be judging my team members for plucking a few heads of wheat when they're hiking through the countryside and they're hungry!"

37

Handicapped Man Welcomed Back Into Society

ON ANOTHER DAY OF REST, I was in Jerusalem for one of the feasts, instructing the people in a local congregation, using very simple terms that they could understand.

"I want to tell you how much it means to be a part of God's spiritual family," I taught them. "Picture a hidden treasure chest full of priceless gold and jewelry buried in a field. One day, a man discovers it and is ecstatic! He quickly re-buries the treasure chest and rushes home to sell everything he owns to be able to buy that field. He purchases it and receives the deed to the land, with full right of possession of all that is on it, including the buried treasure.

"Or picture a wholesale jeweler out looking for quality pearls. One day he finds an exquisite pearl that costs a fortune. He rushes back to his store and liquidates his entire inventory and everything that he has personally to be able to buy that one pearl. When he buys it, he receives the certificate of ownership of that pearl, and has full right of possession.

"Or picture a fishing net. One day some fishermen toss it into the lake and catch a net full of every kind of fish. When the net can't hold any more fish, they pull it in and head back to shore, where they sit down to sort the catch. They drop the good fish into packing crates, ready to go to market, and they toss the bad fish into large trashcans.

"The end of the world will be just like that. The angels will come out and separate the wicked from those who walk with God. They will throw them out of society for being evil. They will toss them into the fires of hell, where they won't be able to stop crying. They will be sick to their stomachs with regret for the choices they made in life.

"Do you understand what I'm telling you?" I asked the congregation. They all nodded respectfully.

"Those of you who are our beloved religious teachers, you love to learn about the way of life God wants for people. You study to be experts in the holy books. You love to record important events and explain the words of God to others. You are like a home-owner who wants to show others the treasures in his house—both the latest novelties, and the antiques that have been in the house for a very long time!"

As I was teaching, I noticed a man whose right hand was crippled. The right hand was considered very important. Whenever a person of high rank put a guest at his right hand, he was giving that person equal honor and dignity. The right hand was also used for giving and receiving. This poor man lived a very lonely life because he couldn't give or receive.

Of course, when the Spiritual Ones and the Realists saw that I noticed the handicapped man, they watched me like hawks to see if I would heal him. They were determined to catch me breaking the law on the Day of Rest, so they could bring charges against me. Some of them became quite argumentative and tried to start a fight.

"Is it lawful to heal on the Day of Rest?" one of them asked, wanting to make me look like a criminal, but I knew exactly what they were thinking.

"Come here, Sir," I ordered the handicapped man. "Stand in the middle of the congregation please." The man obeyed as everyone watched, expectantly. Then I asked the religious experts a question:

"If you had only one precious sheep, and it accidentally fell into a hole on the Day of Rest, would you leave it there to panic and die, or would you grab it and pull it out of there, regardless of the day of the week? You wouldn't sit and wait till the following day! You would save it, wouldn't you? Don't you know that a person is much more valuable than a sheep? Isn't it lawful then to help people in need, even on a holy day?

"You know how specific the holy books are about kindness to animals. Whenever we notice a stray animal, aren't we supposed to catch it and take care of it? If we see a beast of burden wandering around with a heavy load on its back, aren't we supposed to relieve it? And whenever we come across an injured animal, aren't we supposed to nurse it back to health?

"God commands us to take full responsibility for the care and upkeep of any lost or distressed animal until its owner arrives, regardless of whether the owner is a friend, a relative, a stranger, or even an enemy![167]

"So if we're supposed to be kind to animals every day of the week, wouldn't you consider it lawful to do something that helps another human being on the Day of Rest? Or do you think we should look the other way and ignore someone in need because it's more important to be religious?

"Do you consider it legal to rescue people from danger, and heal the sick on the Day of Rest? Or are we supposed to let them die, and effectively commit murder, just so we can fulfill our religious duty? What do you think? Are we supposed to do good on the Day of Rest, or are we supposed to do evil? Restore life, or destroy it?"

Nobody wanted to answer my question. I looked around for anyone in the crowd that would disagree with me, but nobody did. I was furious. I was incredibly saddened by their lack of sympathy and understanding for others. No one was willing to speak up, so I turned to the handicapped man.

"Stretch out your hand!" I ordered him. The man stretched out his crippled right hand towards me, and as he did, it was instantly healed. Now both his hands were normal. The man was thrilled that he could live a healthy life again and participate fully in society. Now he was free to use his right hand to give and receive again!

The so-called religious experts completely overlooked the miracle. They were angry with me and immediately slipped out of the building. When I heard that they were meeting with Governor Herod's people to plan a strategy to kill me for disagreeing with them, I decided to leave Jerusalem and go back home to Galilee.

Many others left Jerusalem and the surrounding areas of Judea and followed us, just to listen to my teachings. Some had heard about my healing the man with the crippled hand, and came from as far away as the Dead Sea, from east of the Jordan River, and from the west coast cities of Tyre and Sidon to find healing for their diseases. They came in huge numbers, with faith that I would touch them and heal them. I healed them all.

Whenever the crowds caught sight of me, they would rush towards me, wanting to touch me—especially the ones who were suffering from serious illnesses. Having heard how I had healed others, they couldn't wait to receive their own miracle.

The demonized people caused even more chaos than the sick, because they would fall down at my feet, sobbing.

"You're the Son of God!" the demons would scream, interrupting my teaching and demanding to be freed from their torment. I ordered the spirits to stop yelling and to quit advertising who I was because the evil spirits always recognized me.

I didn't want to be crushed by the mob, so whenever I was by the lake, I would ask my team members to find me a small boat. Sitting in the boat, I could pull away from the shore and continue to teach and heal.

Whenever I met people who were brokenhearted, or devastated, I would not break them further. If their dreams were smoldering in the ashes of despair, I would not kill their hopes. Instead, I would speak words of truth, firmness and stability to help them become stronger than their problems, and give them the courage to act so that justice would prevail in the end.

Everywhere I went, people of all races and religious backgrounds came, looking to me with great expectation, desire and hope! I set them all free from the demons that held them in their grip, proving by my works that I had the authority and the trust of God to deliver mankind from bondage!

38

Crowds Gather For Hilltop Seminar

BY NOW, I WAS WELL KNOWN for my public service, and I needed to spend some time alone, praying. I took off for the mountains and spent all night in conversation with God. We discussed a lot of important matters. The following morning, I waited for my team members to join me. They had been with me for quite a while now, and were really dedicated to me and my mission.

"Thanks for meeting me here," I said when they arrived. "The time has come for me to pick twelve of you and give you special powers. If I call your name, I want you to step forward and stay here in the mountains with me for a few days of special training." Everyone stood expectantly, wondering if they would be called.

"Simon Peter—you've been a fisherman until now, but I'm going to call you a Rock. Bring your brother, Andrew. Next—James and John—I'm going to call you two the Sons of Thunder.

"Then I want Philip, Bartholomew, and Matthew—yes, the tax collector who has been with us everywhere. Then Thomas; James, the son of Alphaeus; Thaddeus; and Simon, the Zealot. And last but not least, I want you, Judas Iscariot. We need to spend quality time together. I have a lot to share with you. Come up higher with me now.

"I'm going to call the twelve of you my personal representatives," I said. "I want you to be around me all the time, so that you can absorb who I am. You'll be the ones going out on assignments to represent me. I'm going to send you out ahead of me to announce my arrival to the towns and villages we'll be visiting.

"You'll be like mini John-the-Baptists. By the time I send you out, you'll be strong and independent. You'll know me so intimately that you'll be able to use my power and authority to heal the sick and throw demons out of people's lives."

The twelve agreed, but none of them knew that my twelfth representative would one day betray me—not even Judas himself.

My group of personal representatives and I had a wonderful time at our mountaintop retreat. When it was over, we made our way back down to the plains. A huge crowd of people that had followed us on our way home from the feast in Jerusalem was still there, waiting.

When they saw me coming, they rushed towards me, eager to hear my teachings and to be healed. It was obvious that I had to find a place to sit where they could all see me. I decided to walk to the top of a hill. I picked a spot with good visibility, high above them, and sat down to teach. All the rest of my team members were also there, eager to soak up my words.

"Today, I want to talk to you about how much God loves you," I said. "God wants to be in a close, intimate, personal relationship with each one of you. He wants you to be happy; but true joy has absolutely nothing to do with the circumstances in your life going well. Things can be going terribly, and you can still be content! That's because happiness doesn't depend on circumstances at all. True joy comes purely from having a satisfying relationship with God.

"What do you mean, Teacher?" asked an old man in the crowd.

"Even when you don't have the basic needs of life," I explained, "and you are spiritually and emotionally bankrupt, you can still be full of joy, simply because you have God living in you. You may fall on hard times. You may feel hopeless and be in total despair because of all your problems. You may have absolutely nothing left of yourself to hold onto and can only beg for God's help. And yet you can feel peace and be filled with the love and presence of God."

"I know what peace feels like. But how can I have it in the tough times?" the old man wanted to know.

"The prophet Isaiah explained that God doesn't just live in the heavens," I said. "He also lives in you—providing you have a broken heart and truly regret the bad choices you have made in your past. If you humbly look to him, he will refresh and rebuild your spirit.[168]

"He will be with you when you are out of money, or feeling depressed or needy; when your life is full of problems; when you feel discouraged and broken-hearted. All you have to do is to turn to God with respect and sincere reverence.

"That's why even when you are suffering terribly, like when you are mourning the death of a friend or loved one, or experiencing deep inner grief over any kind of loss, you can still be content, because God himself comforts you when you mourn.

He gives you beauty instead of the ashes of death; and joy instead of the heaviness of loss—so that you can see the difference in your life and know that God has done it!"[169]

"How can I experience that comfort when everything seems to be going wrong?" asked a young woman holding a small child.

"If you are willing to accept that God's dealings with you in every situation are good, no matter what the circumstances look like; and if you don't argue with him or resist him, then you'll be full of joy and happiness and you'll inherit God's beautiful earth and all that is in it," I said.

"Young people," I explained, "if you long to please God and obey all of his commandments more than you long for food and drink, you'll be content. You'll experience the deep satisfaction of putting God's word into practice in your life and being pleasing to him. God welcomes the thirsty to come to the waters; and the poor to come and eat. He invites everyone, regardless of race, color or religion, to come and receive the priceless wine and milk of his presence without bringing any money. It's free![170]

"What's more," I continued, still talking to the young people, "God promises that when you experience confusion and disappointment, public humiliation, embarrassment and disgrace; when your emotions are shattered, and your spirit is broken and disillusioned; if you serve God you'll be able to eat and drink and be glad, even when things around you aren't going well at all.

"Here's another way to experience happiness and the blessings of God. Stop being selfish. When God inspires you to notice other people's needs, do something to help them with compassion and kindness, and you'll experience true joy. God will return the favor and be merciful and compassionate to you when you need help one day. You'll end up being blessed when you understand someone else's need and you use good judgment and common sense to respond and help appropriately.[171]

"Look everyone," I said. "God has seven special blessings for you when you are good to the poor. Let me tell you what they are:

God will deliver you in your day of trouble.

He will carefully watch over you and keep you alive.

He will put you on a straight path to success and prosperity on this earth.

He will not allow your enemies to have their way with you.

He will strengthen you in times of sickness and discouragement.

He will be strongly attracted to you and personally protect you, not allowing anyone to harm you or to make fun of you when you are suffering.

Finally, God will keep you whole and put you in a position of authority in his presence forever.[172] Now, who wouldn't want that?"

A young man was looking at me with hope in his eyes.

"If you refuse to pollute your mind with wickedness," I said to him, "your conscience will be clear and you will feel good. That's called being blessed, and that is what true joy is. If you turn your back on evil, you won't have to experience the horrible feelings of guilt that automatically follow wrongdoing. If you keep yourself pure, you will see God, because God is pure.

"Remember that the holy books explain how you can live in God's presence if you live a moral life, do good to others, and speak the truth. If you live a full, meaningful life, and if you're honest and sincere with others, you'll enjoy living before God with a clear conscience."[173]

Turning to a young girl and her sister, I said:

"When you receive the peace of God in your heart, don't just keep it to yourself. Go and make peace between people who hate each other and are refusing to talk to each other. Then you'll experience true happiness. Because when you act as a peacemaker, you show the character of God and he will call you his peacemaking children."

To a young student, I said:

"If anyone keeps annoying you or mocking you because of your commitment to God, consider yourself as special to God. If anyone laughs at you, or persecutes you in any way because you're obeying God, consider yourself really blessed. If anyone ever harasses you or mistreats you because you believe in me, be happy. Remember that God is in you and all the riches and resources of his domain are at your disposal."

As I taught, different people would ask me questions and I would give an illustration or respond with questions to get the students to think. Religious teaching in our day was a very interactive process. The people were eager to listen to my teachings and they freely asked questions about issues that had been bothering them. By the time I finished answering all their questions, they were speechless. They sat in awe and amazement, deep in thought. They could tell that I spoke with authority, which was quite a contrast to the bland and ineffectual way their religious experts taught.

Crowds Gather For Hilltop Seminar

When I finished teaching, I got up to head down the mountain. The enormous crowd lunged forward and rushed after me as if I were a magnet. They had to hurry to keep up with me, but as they chased after me in silence, they continued to think about everything I had told them.

39

Army Officer Asks For Help

I MADE MY WAY DOWN the mountain and back to our haven in Capernaum again. When I arrived at the city gates, the elders were very upset and agitated. They were all there as usual to discuss city business, but as soon as they saw me, they rushed towards me with an urgent request.

"There's a Roman officer stationed here in Capernaum," their leader said. "He's a centurion—a captain over a hundred men. He has a slave who is absolutely devoted to him, but the slave has fallen ill and is at death's door. He's not expected to live through the day!"

Slavery was a common practice throughout the world. Often people who couldn't pay their debts gave up their freedom and offered themselves or their children as payment.

"This officer loves his slave like a son," said another of the elders. "He has heard all about you and begged us to ask you on his behalf. Please, we implore you, come to his house and heal his servant. We want to stress to you that this officer is very deserving of this favor from you. Even though he's in the Roman army, he loves our people. He's the one who built us the new meeting hall that you like to go to for our religious services!" they insisted.

"I'll come and heal him," I said without hesitation.

Army Officer Asks For Help

We were almost at the officer's house when we met his friends, whom he had sent out to look for us.

"Please, Sir, don't trouble yourself to come all the way to the house," one of them insisted. "The officer says that you are of such high rank that he is not worthy for you to come into his house. He doesn't even consider himself deserving enough to bring you this message in person, which is why he sent us, his Hebrew elders and friends."

Then the officer himself came running up to me.

"Sir," he said, "You are a busy man. You shouldn't have to come all the way to my house. I know that if you just give the order, my slave will be healed. He is like a son to me, and he's stuck home in bed, unable to move and in terrible pain.

"Your team members have told me all about your God, and how people have screamed out to him for help when they are desperate, and how he has delivered them from their distress. I've heard how he sent his word and healed them and saved them from destruction,[174] and I've heard that you have God's authority to do miracles.

"You don't have to come all the way to my house. Like you, I understand what it means to be in a position of authority and give orders. I have soldiers under me, and the Roman emperor has given me the right to command them and expect total obedience from them.

"When I tell one of them: 'Go!' he goes! When I tell another: 'Come here soldier!' he comes. And when I tell my servant: 'Do this!' he does it. I don't have to watch them to know that it's done. They do it because of my authority. I don't have to see you come to my house. I know that if you will just give the order, my slave will be healed."

I listened to the officer in amazement at his understanding of the power of authority. I turned to the people that were following me to his house.

"You know, I have never met a person with faith like this among the Hebrews!" I said. "Not even among the most devout religious leaders. This man has total confidence that my order is sufficient to get the job done, and he's not even a Hebrew!

"The prophets foretold that multitudes of people from other cultures all around the world will come to sit down at the heavenly banquet with our ancestor Abraham, and his son Isaac, and his grandson Jacob.[175] God's name will be great around the globe among people who aren't even Hebrews,[176] and in the last days, all nations will come to the mountain of the Lord.[177] Don't you understand that God really meant it when he promised to bless all the families around the world—and not just the Hebrews—because of Abraham?

"But what you don't want to believe is that God will send his real children, the Hebrews, out of his banquet hall and into the extremely dark night, where they will be thrown into the burning flames of hell. There they will live for eternity, weeping bitter tears of regret and kicking themselves for having wasted their lives and not practiced their faith!

"Go home," I said to the officer. "You have believed in your heart that your servant will be healed, and you have spoken it with such confidence, that what you have said will actually be created out of nothing and it will come to pass. It will materialize strictly as a result of your faith!"

The officer's friends who had come out to speak to me went back with him to the house and found that the sick slave was now out of bed. He had completely recovered. They asked him how long he had been feeling well. He told them the time when he took a turn for the better, and they realized that it was at the exact time that I had ordered his healing.

40

Dead Man Walks Again

THE DAY AFTER I HEALED the officer's slave in Capernaum, we went to a town called Nain, about ten miles south of Nazareth. It was built high on Moreh Hill, with a beautiful view across the plains all the way to the mountains in the distance. As usual, many of my team members came with me, and a large crowd of onlookers followed.

Nain didn't have city walls, but it did have gates. As we approached the city gate, we met a large burial procession heading out of town. They were on their way to bury someone in the local cemetery, where the tombs were cut directly in the rocky hills. According to the holy books, God created people from dust, and they return to the dust when they die.[178] The cemetery had to be outside the city so that people would not be contaminated by the dead.

"What's going on?" I asked.

"Oh, Sir," the people wailed. "The only son of a local widow has died tragically. His mother is beside herself with grief!"

A considerable crowd of townspeople was walking with the mother to the cemetery, propping her up in her grief. The young man's body was already covered in spices and ointments and wrapped in linens, ready for burial. Several of his friends were carrying him on an open stretcher.

When I caught sight of the widow, I was really moved by her pain. First, she had lost her husband, and now—her only son!

"Don't cry any more, dear lady," I said with deep compassion. I grabbed the stretcher with a tight grip and the men carrying it immediately came to a standstill.

"Young man," I ordered the dead body, "Get up!" At that, the dead man suddenly sat up.

"Mom? Why are you crying?" he asked. "Guys? What's going on? Set me down. I'm fine! I can walk! Let's go home."

"You see," I told his mother, "you can stop crying now. You have your son back!" The widow was so excited, she could hardly contain herself. The pallbearers set the stretcher down and the young man got up. His mother hugged her son's neck, tears of gratitude and joy running down her face. A feeling of reverence fell over the crowd, and they too started praising and thanking God.

"A great prophet has risen up among us!" they said to each other. "Sir, we see that you have insight into the secrets of God's power and you're able to use that power to help others. This young man's resurrection back to life is living proof that God has come to take care of us, his people, and we are blessed!"

41

The Agony Of Doubt

WHILE I WAS IN GALILEE busily teaching and helping people who had come to me desperate for healing and deliverance, my cousin John was still sitting behind bars in the prison at the fortress of Machaerus, perched dramatically on a hilltop overlooking the Dead Sea.

The fortress was originally built to protect our people from the Nabateans, who lived in the pink rock gorges of Petra, in Jordan, where our Governor's first wife was from. For centuries, everyone had believed it was impossible to attack the fortress; but one day, almost sixty years before I was born, the Romans succeeded in capturing it and they gave Herod the Great orders to hold the position secure.

When Herod the Great arrived at Machaerus, he first built a wall all around the fortress, with tall guard towers in each corner. Then he designed a beautiful summer palace to be built inside the walls. Ironically, it was to this palace that his son's first wife, the Nabatean princess, would flee when she learned that her husband, Herod Antipas, had married another woman while on a visit to Rome.

While my cousin was in prison inside the fortress, from time to time he would receive visitors. His followers would come to tell him about the incredible miracles I was performing in people's lives.

The Agony Of Doubt

At first, John was excited; but the longer he sat there, the more depressed he became. Eventually, sitting all alone, he was attacked by doubts. He had been so sure I was the powerful judge described by the prophet Daniel. Now he wasn't so sure.

"God, why are you letting this happen to me?" he cried out in his cell. "I've been your faithful servant since birth, yet here I am stuck in prison! I feel like something has gone badly wrong with my mission. If my cousin Jesus really is the expected Savior, and if you have given him the power to heal the sick and bring the dead back to life, then why can't I get my miracle? Why doesn't he come and rescue me?"

After weeks of agonizing over this question with no response, John called for two of his closest friends.

"I need you to do something very important for me," he confided in them. "Go and find my cousin Jesus, and ask him specifically if he is the Savior or not?[179] Is he the Peaceful One? Is he the Star of Jacob? Is he the King of Israel?[180] Is he the one that the prophet Isaiah predicted would be coming? Should I stop being afraid and be strong? Has he come to save our people from our enemies? [181] Am I ever going to get out of here?"

When my cousin's two friends tracked me down, I was busy with the crowds. They sat down and waited patiently while I healed the people who were waiting in line for my help. They watched as I touched several blind patients and gave them back their sight. Then I freed a handful of others from the demons that were tormenting them. When I finished, John's friends came to talk to me.

"Sir," one of them said, "your cousin John wants to know whether you're the Savior that we've been expecting for centuries—or will that be someone else in the future?"

I didn't answer their question directly because I understood the real question behind their question. John was wondering why I wasn't acting like the powerful political leader everyone was expecting. Why was I being so humble and staying out of the limelight? And why, if I was doing all these miracles for other people, did I not get him out of prison?

"Go back to John," I said, "and tell him again what you've seen and heard here. Give him examples of how you personally saw blind people recovering their sight and the lame walking again. Tell him that you saw lepers being cleansed and restored back to society, and that you heard deaf and mute people able to hear and talk again. Tell him how the dead are being raised back to life and the poor are hearing good news being announced specifically to them."

"Remind him that the prophet Isaiah predicted that one day the deaf would hear and obey, and the blind would see.[182] God would bring prisoners out from the jail cells of their personal hell and those who sit in the darkness of ignorance and obscurity would be set free.[183] Remind him of the promise that those who look for God would certainly find him." [184]

John would understand my message. He knew that if my healing miracles were real, then I had to be the Savior, because the Savior was supposed to perform amazing miracles of healing.

"Remind John," I told them, "that the prophet also predicted that the Spirit of God would be on me because God has set me apart to preach good news to those willing to obey. He has sent me to bandage up the broken-hearted and to proclaim liberty to those who are in prison and in exile. He has instructed me to tell those who are bound in the chains of mental torment that their prison doors are open.[185]

"Remind him also that the prophet Isaiah wrote that I will be a place of safety for those who trust me for protection and forgiveness; but for those who refuse to obey God, I will be like a sharp rock they will smash into. For them I will be like a brick wall; or a trap door that will open under them. Many in Jerusalem will trip over me or be trapped by my words.[186] But anyone who doesn't consider me to be the trigger on the trap door leading to his ruin will be blessed."

John's messengers thanked me for my answer and headed back to tell him what I had said. As they were leaving, I decided to address the topic of John with the crowds, because many of them had gone out to the Jordan River to be baptized by him.

"When you flocked out to the desert to hear John the Baptist preach, what did you go out to see?" I asked them all. "Did you go to watch a reed on the river bank moving in the wind—like someone who is all talk and no action? Or did you go out to see a man dressed in fine jewelry and designer clothes? You know as well as I do that people with fabulous clothes live in luxurious mansions and regal palaces, and not in the middle of the desert!

"So what did you go out to see? A prophet? A prophet is someone who has insight into the heavenly secrets of God, and is able to clearly communicate those secrets to people on earth. That's who you really went out to see, isn't it? Because John is a real live prophet; in fact, he's much more than a prophet, because God promised he would be the one sent to prepare the way for me.[187]

"Let me tell you a secret: there has never been anyone greater than the prophet John!"

The people were stunned. They knew about many famous prophets and nobody had ever mentioned John.

"Yes," I continued, "from the moment that John started to preach, God's spiritual family suddenly appeared, and the momentum grew, as people sincerely and earnestly began to follow God in every detail of their lives.

"You know that a sheepfold has no door," I explained, "so the shepherd lies down to sleep in the opening to keep the sheep in and the wolves out. In the morning, when the shepherd gets up, the human barrier is gone and the sheep pour out through the opening.[188] The prophet Micah predicted that when John got up to preach, the floodgates would open and the power of belief would rush out like a tsunami, with me as the leader, riding at the front of this tidal wave.[189] John was the one who provided the force and energy for my mission to succeed.

"There is one big difference between John and all the other prophets. John is actually the Elijah who had to come back to lead a dramatic spiritual revival before the Savior's arrival.[190] Isn't that what he has done?

"But here is the amazing news: if you are in God's spiritual family, even the least important one of you will be greater than John!"

The people were overwhelmed by my words. What I was saying was too much for them to grasp.

"What shall I compare this generation to?" I asked them. "You're like children sitting in the playground and calling out to your friends, saying, 'Come on! We've played happy flute music for you but you don't want to dance! We've played sad funeral music and cried for you, but you don't want to mourn!'

"When you saw how disciplined John was, living in austerity, neither eating rich food nor drinking wine, you said that he was demon-possessed! Now I have come, eating and drinking and enjoying life, and you say I'm a glutton and a drunk! You're upset that I like to spend my free time around tax collectors, gangsters and prostitutes!

"But those of you who are wise are able to see the real truth about why I am here. So what is it going to take for you to act? If you are willing to hear what I have to say, then seriously think about my teachings, and put them into practice!" I challenged them.

42

The Secret Of Contentment

"GOD'S SPIRITUAL FAMILY is now open to all," I announced as I walked from village to village, "no matter your racial or moral background!" Everywhere I went, I demonstrated my good news by performing many miracles and healing all the people who came to me for help.

My twelve special representatives were with me every step of the way. Also with us were several women who had been healed and set free from demonic spirits, including Mary Magdalene. When I set her free, seven demons had come out of her! Joanna was from the royal palace, the wife of a high-ranking steward in Governor Herod Antipas' court. Susanna also came with us on our travels, as did many others. They all supported me with their time and their finances, sharing whatever they had at their disposal—be it property, money or other worldly goods.

I warned them all that tough times were coming.

"Over the centuries there have been some really wicked cities," I told them. "Sodom and Gomorrah, Tyre and Sidon, Nineveh—just to name a few. But even the people of Nineveh repented as soon as the prophet Jonah came and preached to them.[191]

"Now, in contrast, look at the towns where I've performed my amazing miracles. Take Chorazin, just outside Capernaum, for example! And Bethsaida, on the north-east coast of Lake Galilee! These are two extremely prosperous towns. Everyone has heard of their famous shipyards and fish processing plants. Everyone has heard of their leather and fabric dyeing factories, where they take thousands of sea shells to produce just one ounce of purple dye.

"But even though these wealthy people have seen me heal their sick friends and family members with their own eyes, they have not turned to God. They are proud and ungrateful. They live like they don't need God for anything.

"If the shameless people of the ancient island city of Tyre, not to mention the wicked souls in the Lebanese port of Sidon, had seen all my miracles, they would have begged God for forgiveness. You know, it will be more tolerable for Tyre and Sidon on the Day of Judgment than for Chorazin and Bethsaida.

"Let's take another example—beautiful Capernaum on the sparkling waters of Lake Galilee, where I've spent so much time and done so many great things. The people of Capernaum love their huge mansions and their large courtyards and patios; they consider themselves superior because they live on the main road to Damascus in Syria. They are counting on the city's fine reputation to reach as high as heaven and save them from God's punishment!

"But their pride will pull them all the way down to Hades, where the spirits of the dead live. They will fall just like the great archangel Lucifer, whose pride caused him to fall from heaven itself.[192]

"If the wicked people of Sodom had seen the miracles I performed in Capernaum recently, they would never have been destroyed by fire! If the people of Capernaum could only see the presence of God in the great miracles they are experiencing, they would turn back to God! But if not, when the Day of Judgment comes, the people of Sodom will get a lighter sentence than the people of Capernaum!"

I stopped teaching for a minute and prayed out loud.

"Thank you, God, for your brilliant strategy. There are dozens of security guards patrolling city walls around the world, looking for suspicious activity. There are hundreds of learned astronomers and scientists searching the night sky for signs. There are thousands of wise men and women studying the holy books for clues about the coming Messiah. But you have purposely hidden your brilliant strategy from them all.

"Instead, you have chosen to expose the secrets of the supernatural world to ordinary people who simply trust you. Instead of the powerful, you have chosen the powerless to establish your power on earth. Instead of great spiritual leaders, you have decided to use beginners to open the doors to your spiritual community to others."[193]

I paused, and looked at all the people.

"The reason I just prayed," I explained to them, "is because you can know my father, just as I do. I'm revealing the supernatural God to you. He is my father and he has given me everything that exists. He is the only one who really knows me and I am the only one who really knows him, which is why I can do this for you. So come to me if you're struggling with the issues of life, or if you're overwhelmed by all your problems. I'll refresh you and give you rest.

"You know how a farmer puts a wooden framework, called a yoke, over the heads of two oxen, to link them together so they can pull carts with heavy loads? My stepfather was a carpenter. I know all about yokes and oxen.

"I know that the farmer yokes the youngest, most inexperienced ox with the gentlest and most patient older one, so they can train by walking together side by side. Well, I want you to slip into my yoke with me and learn from me, because I'm humble. I'll walk you gently and steadily through your day. With me at your side, you'll find complete rest for your souls.

"I won't make you push or pull faster than you're able to go. When you walk through your day with me, you'll stop rushing around stirring up a lot of dust and achieving little. I'll set the pace and you'll see what it's like to experience life through my eyes.

"Then you'll discover what it feels like to stop struggling and start relaxing as we make our way through life together. Because the yoke I put on you is custom-fitted and very comfortable; and the load I give you to carry is feather-light, because I'm pulling it along with you. Of course, if you try and get ahead of me, you'll feel all the weight on your shoulders. But if you relax and walk beside me, everything will be fine!

"As the prophet Jeremiah said: 'Ask for the good path and walk in it, and you will find rest in that inner, private part of yourself that is the real you, the part that longs for peace.'"[194]

43

A Precious Gift From An Unlikely Source

SIMON, ONE OF THE LOCAL Spiritual Ones, invited me to spend some quality time with him over a home-cooked meal. I was happy to accept his invitation and went over to his house for dinner. Comfortable cushions were set out on the floor for us to lean on, and bowls of delicious food were brought out by the ladies in his family. Several members of his household joined us and quietly listened as we talked.

Suddenly, I felt something at my feet. A woman had come up behind me, fallen to the ground, and grabbed me by the feet. She was sobbing as if her heart was about to break. Her tears were pouring down onto my feet and she kept kissing them and wiping them with her long hair.

When Simon, my host, saw what was going on, he was disgusted. *"She's the local whore!"* he thought. *"How on earth did she get into the house? How embarrassing! Everyone in town knows her, even the foreigners who come through town! There's no telling what she'll reveal! Whoever let her slip through the front door is going to pay for this outrage!"*

The sobbing woman opened up an alabaster box that was shaped like a beautiful vase filled with expensive sweet-smelling ointment. She dipped her fingers into the perfumed ointment and began to massage it into my feet. It felt good on my tired and achy feet.

Simon had specifically invited me to come and be alone with him in the privacy of his home when this woman showed up out of nowhere and without invitation. *"If Jesus were a real prophet,"* Simon was thinking to himself, *"he would have realized who this woman is, and what kind of life she's involved in! He'd know that she is totally unacceptable in good company, and absolutely unfit to be touching him, because she is such trash!"*

I knew what was going through Simon's mind, so I said, "Simon, I have something to share with you."

"Go ahead, Sir," Simon said respectfully, leaning forward eagerly to hear what I had to say.

"I want to tell you a story," I said. "Once upon a time there was a man who was owed money by two different debtors. The first debtor owed him five hundred coins, and the second one owed him fifty. Neither of them was able to pay him back, so frankly, he was kind enough to forgive them both. Now I have a question for you—which of the two was more grateful and loved him the most?"

Simon was quick to respond.

"Obviously the first debtor, who was forgiven the larger amount!"

"You're absolutely correct, Simon," I said. "Now let's apply this principle to what just happened here. When I arrived at your house and took off my sandals, you, my host, didn't give me the customary water to wash my tired, dusty feet and get comfortable before we sat down to eat. But look at this woman, Simon—she's a complete stranger—yet she has washed my feet with her tears and wiped them with her hair!

"When I walked in your door, you didn't give me a welcome kiss to show your affection for me; but she hasn't stopped kissing my feet since the time she got here!

"You didn't massage my head with soothing olive oil to help me relax after my trip; but she has massaged my feet with one of the rarest and most expensive perfumes a woman could own! She did what God himself does. He prepares a banquet table before us in the presence of our enemies. He pours olive oil on our head and our cup runs over…[195]

"Here's what I'm going to do about this incident, Simon. This woman has a long history of sinning, we all know that. But guess what? Because of how she has treated me, I have forgiven her all her wrongdoing, and so has God! She is totally released from the punishment for her sin because she loves me with all her heart.

"She has expressed her love by bringing me the very best she has. That perfume is worth about a year's wages. People like you, who haven't been forgiven much, don't love that much either."

I looked back down at the woman.

"All your sins have been forgiven," I said.

The people who were sitting around eating with me began to wonder who I was, and who gave me the power to forgive sins! But I just kept talking to the woman.

"Your faith has delivered you from your past and saved you for a wonderful new future. Go home now and be at peace."

44

A Spectacular Exorcism

ONE DAY, WHILE I WAS back at the log cabin on the mountain training my twelve personal representatives, word spread that we were inside. A large number of people crowded in on us, to the point that we couldn't even sit down to eat.

A delegation arrived with a man who was demon-possessed. The devil had him so bound that he was blind and couldn't see a thing. Worse yet, he was also mute and couldn't speak. I cast out the demons and healed the man on the spot. He was immediately able to see and talk, and the people were absolutely astounded.

"This miracle-worker must be descended from King David himself!" some of them exclaimed. "He must be, since he's able to free people from evil spirits and heal them like that!"

Not everyone was convinced. The Spiritual Ones heard what was being said. They had followed me up from Jerusalem to watch what I did, in case I slipped up.

"We think he's full of Beelzebub—the lord of the flies and the prince of demonic beings—Satan himself! He's casting devils out of people by using the power of Satan himself!" they said with an air of superiority.

I knew exactly what these professors were thinking. I invited them over so we could examine their allegation together. My friends and family thought I was crazy! They tried to talk me out of a potential confrontation, but I wanted to have an open discussion with my opponents.

"Let me get this straight," I said. "You're saying that I'm on Satan's side and it's through his power that I just cast the devil out of a mute blind man? That doesn't make any sense at all! If Satan is the ultimate of evil spirits, the one who comes between friends and accuses people to God, why would he throw himself out of this man? He would be giving up his own territory!"

"Let me give you an illustration. If there's serious division in a country, and people turn on each other, it leads to civil war. That country can't survive when its people are fighting each other. It's destined for destruction and ruin, isn't it?

"By the same token, if the residents of a city are divided into two warring camps, that community will be torn apart. And if family members start a quarrel that leads to a family feud, the love and the bond in that family are broken. It's logical then, that if Satan starts a war against himself, his domain will collapse and his end will come.

"By the way, if what you're saying was actually true, and I did cast out demons by the power of Satan, then by whose authority are your children casting out evil spirits? Because some of them are, aren't they? You would have to accuse your own children of the same thing, because your argument cuts both ways. I guarantee you that if you accused your kids of such an evil, they would judge you and turn on you in a real hurry!

"But back to what you're saying. What if I'm actually casting out devils through the power of God? That would mean that God's spiritual community has come very close to you! Don't you remember that Pharaoh's magicians were not able to copy all the miracles God did through Moses?[196] What if God is doing this through me? If he is, then wouldn't it be true that God's power is being demonstrated right here among you?

"Don't you remember that the prophet Daniel predicted that the God of heaven would set up a community that would never be destroyed? It would smash and consume all other empires, even the domain of darkness, with all its demons, and it would stand forever.[197]

"But let's get practical and look at this on an individual level. What if a strong man is armed with weapons and protected by armed guards and a fail-safe security system? He feels secure and he doesn't have to worry about his possessions, does he?

"But if an even stronger man wants to break into the man's house and steal all his belongings, does he not first have to take out all the guards and the security system? Then he has to overpower the strong man and tie him up to neutralize him, so he can't move. Only then can he steal the wealthy man's possessions and divide them up among his friends and relatives.

"In the same way, I first had to get rid of the evil spirit controlling the mute blind man, before I could heal him and set him free to follow the path of God. If the power of God is working through me, then I'm stronger than Satan.

"If I want to help a person in need, first I have to take out the demons that are controlling him. Only then can I go in and meet his needs—and that's what you should be doing instead of standing around and criticizing me after the fact!

"If you're not helping me and working with me, you're actually being obstructive and working against me. It's as simple as that. If you're not inviting people into God's community with me, you're actually scattering them farther from his reach!"

Some of them continued to protest.

"You have a demon in you," they insisted.

"You may not like the fact that I performed this miracle," I said, "but if you deny the power of God behind the miracle and say that I have a demon, as your professors are doing, then you're calling the spirit of God a demon, and God will never forgive you.

"Mark my words," I said to them. "You can be forgiven for any sin that you might ever commit—any act of disobedience to God's law—even if you're guilty of abusing someone in the most vicious way by using false witnesses to lie about him and ruin his reputation, which, by the way, is the very worst type of lie!

"If you say bad things about me, you can be forgiven. But if you ever speak evil of God's holy Spirit, the very breath of God, and hurt his reputation or resist him when he's touching your heart and persuading you to turn back from your evil ways, you'll never be forgiven for what you've said, neither in this world nor in the world to come.

"Let me explain why. God respects your free will. If you insist on resisting the convincing power of the holy Spirit of God that is leading you to reconsider your ways and turn back to God, you can never be forgiven. Not by God; and not by me. You'll be continually found guilty and you'll be destined for eternal damnation—a sentence of total separation from God and from all that is wonderful forever—by your own choice!

"You've probably heard me use the example of fruit before. You can tell what kind of a tree you have by looking at the fruit it produces. If you see an orange, it's logical to assume that it grew on an orange tree, and not on a poisonous berry tree. If you see good fruit, it's logical that it grew on a good tree. If you see someone living a good life, then it's logical to assume that you're looking at a good person. If you see someone living a bad life, then it's logical to assume that you're looking at a bad person.

"You should be looking at the results I'm producing to decide what kind of a person I am, just as I'm listening carefully to what you're saying, to see what kind of people you are.

"You may not have thought about it before, but your words, as well as your deeds, are your fruit. The words that come out of your mouth are actually the product of what's in your heart, mind and emotions. If you're a good person, your heart overflows with kind words. If you're an evil person, your heart spews out evil words.

"When I listen to what you're saying, I have to conclude that you're a bunch of snake-oil salesmen! You are wicked, malicious and perverse! Instead of being thrilled for the man who is now able to see and talk, you'd rather he still be miserable! You're always planning shrewd twists and you delight in others' tragedies. When your mind is full of scheming and skepticism, how can you possibly speak words that are kind, useful or profitable to others?

"Listen carefully to what I'm telling you here, because you're going to have to account for every idle word that you've ever spoken—even the words that you've blurted out without thinking.

"On the Day of Judgment, when all men stand before God at the end of time, you'll have to answer for everything that you've ever said. So be aware of every word that comes out of your mouth; because the words that you've spoken throughout your lives will be used either to prove your innocence and set you free, or to prove your guilt and sentence you to eternal damnation."

"Sir," said a spokesperson for the religious lawyers and Spiritual Ones, "if you say you didn't cast the evil spirit out using the power of Satan, then by whose power did you cast it out? Why don't you show us a sign to prove who you really are? We'd like that!"

"You know what?" I replied, "Instead of being happy that I set the man free from the grip of evil, you're harassing me! Your question just proves to me that you're evil and very far from God. In fact, you're magicians and adulterers, because they are the kind of people who demand proof! Sorcerers always want some magical sign. Cheaters are always suspicious of others and want proof.

"The only sign you're going to get from me, is the sign of the prophet Jonah. Remember how God called him to go and preach to the wicked people in Nineveh, who worshipped the goddess Ishtar?" I said. "Nineveh was one of the wealthiest cities on the main trade route between east and west. But Jonah refused to obey God and ran in the opposite direction! So God made sure that Jonah was swallowed by a great fish![198]

"You remember how Jonah was in the belly of that fish for three days before he was spat out? The sign that you will see is this: I too will spend three days in dark places. I won't be in the belly of a fish. I'll be in the heart of the earth, in hell itself."

They looked at me with a puzzled look.

"There's a difference between you and the people of Nineveh," I challenged them. "When Jonah eventually arrived in Nineveh and started preaching the coming judgment of God, the people stopped and examined their past. Overcome with regret, they believed Jonah. All of them, from the youngest to the oldest, fasted and cried out to God to forgive their evil ways. You, on the other hand, have someone greater than Jonah here, but you're not turning back to God with humble hearts.

"Let me give you another example from history. Remember the African Queen of Sheba, the ruler of the Sabaean people of Yemen and Ethiopia, who were famous for their trade in precious stones, incense and slaves? She went to a great deal of trouble to find God.

"When she heard that King David's son, the great King Solomon, was super-wise and knew God intimately, she traveled for weeks from south of Aswan, in Egypt—one of the farthest corners of the known world. She sailed down the Nile on barges with her royal attendants, and then crossed the hot desert on camels carrying costly spices, precious stones, and four and a half tons of gold to give to the king.[199]

"When the Queen of Sheba arrived in Jerusalem, she first presented Solomon with her precious gifts. Then she put him through a tough stress test by asking him some very hard questions. She opened up to him and shared everything that was in her heart, including her most difficult personal issues and legal questions, and Solomon satisfied her with his wisdom.[200]

"You have someone much greater than King Solomon here, but you don't go to any great lengths to listen, nor do you open up and share in sincerity what is truly on your hearts while you have the opportunity. All you want to do is trip me up! At the Last Judgment, the Queen of Sheba will stand up and condemn you for not paying attention to the wisdom of God when you had the opportunity!

"But let's go back to the issue at hand," I continued. "We were talking about the mute blind man who was possessed by the devil and who is now completely well and free. Here's an important question. Where do you think the evil spirit went?"

Nobody said a word, so I answered the question for them.

"Remember how God asked Satan once where he had been, and Satan told him that he'd been going back and forth across the earth, and walking up and down in it?[201] When an evil spirit comes out of a human being, it is suddenly left homeless. It wanders through deserted places, looking for a new home where it can rest from all its hard work, but it can't find anything.

"Eventually, the wandering evil spirit gives up and says, 'I think I'll just turn around and go back to my original home. It was nice and familiar there.' When it arrives, it finds the home empty, and all cleaned up and re-decorated. Excited to find it all looking so nice, it goes off and invites seven other spirits of a different quality that are much more wicked than the original one.

"You know of course, that in our culture, the number seven means perfection. So it invites the perfect number of evil spirits to come and live with it. They all rush back into that house and move in to live there permanently. The resulting condition of that person is much worse than in the beginning. That is exactly what it will be like for you and the people of your generation because of your distrust and unbelief!"

By this time, a huge crowd had gathered and was listening in to the conversation. As I was talking, a woman who was sitting in the group became all choked up with emotion.

"Your mother is so lucky to have had the joy of carrying you and bringing you into the world and breast-feeding you!" she cried out dramatically.

"That's not true," I said, unmoved. "The fortunate ones are those of you who hear the word of God and put it into practice in your everyday lives. That's where the great blessing is!"

Just then, a man pushed his way through the crowds.

"Teacher, your mother says she's here with your brothers and sisters," he said. "They've sent me to tell you that they've been standing outside the log cabin waiting to see you but they can't get in because of the crowd! They want you to come out so they can talk to you."

"My mother and my siblings are outside?" I asked. "Wait a minute. You don't understand. Who do you think is my real mother? And who do you think are my real brothers and sisters?"

I looked around at all my followers who were crammed in a circle around me, hanging on my every word. They weren't just listening to me. They were eagerly putting into practice everything I taught them. I stretched out my hand to them and said:

"Meet my real mother and my real brothers and sisters! You're it! If you listen to the words of God and do what my father in heaven requires in his word, you're automatically my real brothers, sisters and mother. I have inherited God's character, and by following me, you have inherited mine, and we're family!"

45

The Pre-requisite For Miracles

THAT SAME DAY I LEFT the cabin in the mountains and went down to Lake Galilee near the Golan Heights. Huge crowds from every town in the area gathered around me, so again, I got into a boat and sat down to teach them. The people all stood on the shore, listening. I decided to explain what God's spiritual family is like using stories about natural things. That day, I told them this story about a farmer:

"Once upon a time," I began, "there was a farmer who went out to sow his seeds. As he tossed the seeds into the ground, some fell by the side of the road. As soon as his back was turned, birds swooped down and snapped the little seeds right up, and people who came along trampled on the seeds left behind by the birds.

"Other seeds fell on rocky ground, which didn't hold enough moisture to water the seeds. The seeds couldn't grow any roots because there was so little topsoil. They immediately sprouted upwards, but then the sun came up and burned the sprouts. They withered away because they didn't have any roots to store extra water and keep them strong.

"Other seeds fell among thorn bushes and prickly wild grass, so thorns and thistles grew up around the new sprouts and choked them before they could produce any fruit.

"But some of the seeds fell on rich soil, known to be fertile land. The seeds grew deep down and developed strong roots. When their shoots sprang up, they grew tall and eventually multiplied. Some produced thirty times more fruit than normal, some sixty, and some a hundred.

"So you see that the seeds were all the same, but the soil where they fell was different. If you understand what I'm saying, listen carefully and apply my teachings to your own lives and you'll know exactly what I'm talking about!"

Later on, when I was alone, my twelve representatives and those who were traveling with me wanted me to explain the story about the seeds.

"You didn't get it, did you?" I said. "If you don't understand this story, how will you be able to understand all the other stories I have to share?"

"Tell us what it means," they begged me. "Who is the farmer, and what's the point you are making?"

"I'm the farmer," I said. "I go out to plant seeds, which are the truths of God. I reach into my heart and speak out the words of God, just like the farmer reaches into his sack and throws out a handful of seeds.

"Some of the seeds fall by the side of the road where there is no topsoil at all; only gravel. If you hear my words and don't have enough background information to be able to understand what they mean, my words won't have any impact on you.

"Because Satan's mission is to steal from you and kill and destroy you, he comes immediately and snatches the word out of your mind to prevent you from believing it and being saved from deception.

"Then there are the seeds that fall on stony ground. You may understand God's word and love to hear about him. At first you may receive his word with gladness and enthusiasm. You may even pray daily, and delight to know his ways.[202]

"But your excitement won't last. If you don't put down any roots in yourselves by applying the word to your lives, you won't have any depth or stabilizing power and your commitment will only be temporary. When troubles and temptations come, you'll quickly fall away.

"The minute someone criticizes you, or laughs at you, or discriminates against you, or persecutes you for your beliefs, you'll be embarrassed. You'll decide that it's better to look good to others than to please God, and you will end up withdrawing from the faith.

"Or when problems and difficulties come up in your life, you'll get distracted and lose your focus on God and forget everything you heard. That's why if you have no depth of understanding, you'll immediately collapse and lose your faith when troubles come. The words of God never produce any results in situations like these.

"Then there are the seeds which fall on thorny ground, where the prickly grass and thistles grow. You may hear the word, but as soon as you walk away, three things can happen:

"First, you may run into personal problems and get distracted and bogged down. You'll start to worry about your own situation and get depressed and completely forget the words of faith.

"Second, you may get excited about material riches and lose your focus on God. Instead of living for him, you'll try to make money and get ahead at any cost, even if you have to compromise your moral standards.

"Or third, you may allow yourself to be seduced by your natural desire for the pleasures of this world. You may decide to pursue your own goals and follow your own wants and needs—even if it means disobeying the very words of God you have been given.

"Just as thistles grow up in the middle of the crops before anyone can notice, these distractions can creep in and choke what you've heard about God, so that it never comes to fruition.

"Seeds are supposed to grow into plants that produce fruit. The word of God is supposed to grow in your lives to produce more believers with the character of God; but if that process is interrupted, the desired end will never be achieved. That's why God instructed the prophet Jeremiah not to sow his seed among thorns.[203]

"Finally, we come to the seeds that are sown on good ground. This soil is rich and fertile and great for growing crops. It has been properly prepared. It has been broken up and then allowed to lie fallow, so that it can restore itself with water and minerals, and be ready to nourish the seeds that fall on it.

"You may be basically a good person—honest and hardworking, with a good heart. When you hear the word of God, you welcome it with open arms and immediately understand what it means. You believe it and eagerly act on it. You keep on patiently believing and putting it into practice regardless of the cost. Even when you face difficult circumstances, you continue to practice it.

"Just as a seed grows into a tree producing lots of fruit, you will grow strong and produce good results. Just as a single physical seed can produce thirty, sixty or even a hundred pieces of fruit, you, a single true believer, can produce thirty, sixty or even a hundred other believers."

"Now I get it!" said one of my friends. "But why do you have to make it so complicated? Why do you have to use stories when teaching the crowds, instead of just telling it like it is?" he asked.

"I like to use stories because they help make the point and they really impact those who are eager to learn. There are plenty of others in the crowd who are just hanging around to see what sensational thing will happen next. But they aren't really paying attention to my teachings. They have no interest in spiritual growth and they are not willing to put out any effort to understand what I am saying, so when they hear me talking, they are confused and unable to understand what I am talking about. They think that I'm talking in riddles; but those who genuinely want to know will understand," I explained.

"The holy books said that I would tell stories and explain things which have been kept secret from the foundation of the world.[204] When I talk about living in God's community and experiencing God's supernatural lifestyle, I'm telling you something that you're naturally ignorant about. You have to have a revelation or an explanation so you can experience what it means to apply God's way of thinking. That's why I like to use stories to demonstrate heavenly truths in earthly terms."

My listeners were intrigued.

"I'm giving those of you who really want to know God the ability to learn to know him. Because if you really want to know him, he'll open your minds and give you an even greater wealth of understanding; but if you don't have a hunger for God, you'll find that even the little understanding you have may slip away from you through lack of interest," I explained.

"Many of you have come here to be entertained by me, or to get something from me, or to criticize me—but not necessarily to follow me," I said. Some of the people looked down in embarrassment. "You're really not interested in following God and actually obeying him," I continued, "and God can see right through you! That's why you will not be given the gift of understanding, and that's why I tell these truths in story form.

"You may see me with your physical eyes, but you don't understand what I'm talking about. You may hear me with your physical ears, but you don't understand what I mean, because if you did, you would already have turned back to God and had all your sins forgiven.

"But this is nothing new!" I said. "Several of the ancient prophets were called by God to speak to people who would end up rejecting their message because they were hard hearted. Ezekiel and Isaiah, for example, had the frustrating assignment of speaking to people, even though they knew that their listeners had absolutely no intention of obeying God.

"The people out there today are just like them!" I explained. "Their hearts have become hardened to what God wants them to feel; their ears have become indifferent to what God wants them to hear; and their eyes have become tired of what God wants them to see. If they could really feel and hear and see, they would be turning back to God, and he would restore them to a healthy relationship with him.

"You, on the other hand, are watching me eagerly and listening intently to what I'm saying, and you are blessed; not because your circumstances are any different than theirs, but because God's Spirit is moving in you, making you sensitive to him.

"Many prophets and holy men and women in the past have walked with God, and longed to see what you're seeing, and to hear what you're hearing, but they haven't had that privilege.

"You, on the other hand, have a beautiful opportunity with me here today. If you walk in my light, you will be a light to others, just like the sun is to the earth. Sunlight is never turned on or off by human hands; it never stops shining. The eternal light of God is lighting you up continuously, so you, also, should never stop shining. The holy books say that the path of the just is as the shining light that shines more and more until the perfect day.[205] Your lives should grow brighter and brighter, as sunlight does from the first rays of dawn to the bright midday.

"Let me tell you why. A city on a hilltop can't possibly be hidden from view, and you shouldn't be hidden either. In fact, your life should shine brighter and brighter continuously, because you are founded and built on the rock for everyone to see.

"When you're at home and it's dark, you light a candle, don't you? You set it up high on a candlestick so that it can light up the whole house for everyone in it. You don't prop it up under an overturned bucket, do you? No. That would be crazy!

"You should be like a candle lighting up this dark world for others. Let your light shine into the dark corners. Expose the darkness so that everyone can see what's really there. Then they will recognize the good that you're doing for others and understand what's really going on, and they will be grateful to God in heaven for what you are doing for them."

When I finished telling them these stories, I left the area, and everyone had a lot to think about.

46

Crew Panics As Boat Takes On Water

"LET'S GO TO THE OTHER side of Lake Galilee," I said to my team members one evening when I saw the huge crowds all around us.

I boarded one of the boats while my team members dismissed the crowds. Some of my followers got into the same boat as I did. Others bobbed along in other little boats. As our party sailed across the lake, I took a nap. Someone gave me a pillow and I fell into a deep sleep in the back of the boat.

Lake Galilee is known for its sudden storms. Whenever cold air rushes down from snow-covered Mt. Hermon and through the gorges in the valley, it collides with the warm air over the lake and causes the waters to swell.

While I was sleeping, a tremendous wind arose and a storm broke out, separating us from the other boats. The waves started beating dangerously against the sides of the boat and splashing all over everybody. Then the boat started to fill with more and more water until it looked like it was going to sink. My team members were desperate. They scrambled over to me and woke me up.

"Sir!" they screamed over the noise of the wind and the waves, "Don't you care that we're about to drown? Save us! We're going under!"

Crew Panics As Boat Takes On Water

"Why are you so afraid?" I asked them. "Where is your faith? How is it that you have no confidence in God?" I stood up in the boat and sharply scolded the wind and the rough waters.

"Settle down," I ordered them. "Be calm. Be still!" Immediately, the wind and the waves died down and there was a great calm. My followers were still terrified by the ordeal, but amazed that I had calmed the storm.

"What kind of a man is he, that even the winds and the waves obey him?" they asked each other.

47

Homeless Man Ruins Local Economy

WE FINISHED CROSSING THE LAKE and arrived within view of the other side, where the slopes of the eastern highlands fall dramatically down to the lake shore. Gadara, about five miles away, was the closest town of the Decapolis, the League of Ten Cities east of the Jordan River. Each of these boom towns had about 15,000 inhabitants, its own currency, its own court system and its own military.

Gadara was one of the most fortified of the ten cities. It was built on a steep hill overlooking some natural hot springs. It was a very civilized and prosperous town, with temples, theatres and impressive public buildings. A growing community, it was composed mainly of the descendants of Greeks who had fled their homes when Alexander the Great invaded. These refugees had done very well in their new life in Gadara and the economy of the town was exploding.

There was only one problem. A crazy local man had everyone in the region terrorized.

"See that man watching us from the vantage point up on that hill?" one of my team members asked me. "We need to be really careful, because he runs around naked and sleeps in the cliffs above the cemetery. He's a local boy, but he lives like a homeless man. He's completely out of control. Nobody is able to restrain him, not even with chains!

"I know the area," my friend told me, "and I can tell you that he has been possessed for many years. The demons often grab him and thrash him around physically. Sometimes he is fiercely aggressive. Other times he is deeply depressed and spends his days and nights screaming and crying and cutting himself with sharp stones.

"I know his family, and I feel so sorry for them. They keep trying to catch him and bring him back. His father and brothers have to grab him and hold him down and then tie him up with iron chains to put his clothes back on; but he always manages to pry open the links in the chain with his fingers and to smash them in pieces. Then the demons drive him back out into the wilds where he rips off his clothes again and hides out in the cemetery!

"The man's poor parents are devastated. In fact, it's to the point now that we're all afraid to travel down the road past the cemetery because he's so aggressive that he could attack us. He hides up there in the caves, which are honeycombed with little chambers cut out of the soft limestone hills, and we never know where he might pop up."

Sure enough, as soon as I stepped out of the boat, the tormented man started running down the hill towards me, waving his arms frantically.

"Watch out! Here comes the wild man!" yelled my team members, obviously panicking. As he got closer, we could hear him yelling and we saw that he was completely naked. He was clearly possessed by evil spirits.

"You're Jesus!" the wild man screamed over and over as he ran toward me. "You're the son of the Most High God! We have absolutely nothing in common with each other!"

I could feel the people's terror. The wild man rushed up to me and fell at my feet in awe.

"Evil spirit!" I commanded the demon inside him. "Come out of this man!"

"Have you come to torment us ahead of schedule?" the spirit asked in a sickly voice. "I'm serious. In God's name, stop tormenting us, I beg of you!"

"What's your name?" I asked the spirit.

"My name is Legion!" snarled the demon. "I'm like the legion in the Roman army with up to six thousand troops, because there are thousands of us that have come to live in here! Don't order us away from this area and into the bottomless pit! We're familiar with this place and we like it here! We're on a mission to push this man to destroy himself. In fact, we are determined to drive him crazy! Please don't send us away. But if you've come to expel us, at least send us into that huge herd of pigs that's feeding near the mountain close by. We don't want to leave the area!"

"That's fine!" I said. "You have my permission to go into the pigs!"

At that, all the evil spirits jumped out of the wild man and entered into the herd of about two thousand pigs that were nearby. As soon as the demons got into the pigs, the whole herd stampeded and rushed down a steep hill. When they got to the water's edge, they just kept on charging into the lake until they drowned!

The employees who were supposed to be looking after the pigs just stood there, powerless to stop the stampede. When they realized that the whole herd was dead, they ran away. They didn't want to be held responsible for the loss. The locals were in shock and awe. They all scattered in fear and went their separate ways, but they told everyone in town and in the countryside what had happened to the demon-possessed man.

"Thank God," said an older woman who had seen the whole thing. "We can all be safe now! Thank you, God, for what you have done for him, and for us!"

When the news reached downtown Gadara, about five miles away, people rushed back out to the lake to take a look at the horrific scene. The bloated bodies of two thousand dead pigs were floating in the water. Even devout Hebrews, who don't eat pork, came to see what had happened. Some of the people who had actually seen the whole drama stayed behind to give blow-by-blow explanations to everyone who came to look.

"See those dead pigs?" they said. "The naked guy was full of demons. Then this Jesus from Nazareth showed up and sent the demons into the pigs—and look what happened! The pigs rushed into the lake, and the crazy guy is perfectly fine now. He's been set free!"

Word spread quickly, and soon the whole town came out to meet me, including people from the surrounding area. Many of them knew the guy. When they arrived, they saw him sitting calmly at my feet, fully clothed and talking and acting normally. Then they saw the bloated carcasses floating in the water, and they panicked.

"This could happen to any one of us!" said a local businessman.

When they heard him, the other business owners were gripped with a tremendous fear, wondering if their company might be put out of business if I stayed. They held a meeting with me and several of them asked me to please leave, before any more wealthy farmers suffered damage. Gadara was a prestigious and prosperous city. They couldn't afford any scandal that would negatively affect the economy.

As I was getting back into the boat, the man who had been demon-possessed begged to stay with me.

"Please let me go with you wherever you go!" he pleaded.

"No," I said. "Go home to your former friends and share with them the awesome things that God has done for you. They know what you were like when you were demon-possessed. Show them how God has had compassion on you and how your life is now completely changed."

So the man took off and began to tell people in Gadara and the other cities in the Decapolis area the great things that I had done for him. When they saw him fully clothed and heard his story, the people were all absolutely amazed at what had happened. He was completely transformed. He had gone from depression, mental illness, suicidal tendencies, violent outbursts and self-mutilation to a calm and normal life the instant I ordered the evil spirits to leave him.

48

Sick Woman Interrupts Rescue Mission

WE GOT INTO OUR BOATS and sailed from Gadara back across Lake Galilee. When we arrived on the opposite shore, a large crowd was already gathered there, eagerly waiting for me. As our boat approached land, the people rushed forward to hug me and welcome me to their town. Unlike the wealthy business people of Gadara, they all wanted to hear my teaching.

"Let me tell you the secret of how God's spiritual family spreads from heart to heart," I taught them. "You can't see growth. You just see the results. Think of it this way; when a woman becomes pregnant, approximately nine months later a baby is born. The woman can't see it growing and she doesn't have any idea how it grows, but it does. Nobody sees it happening; but the baby develops and eventually comes out when it's ready.

"In the same way, when a farmer deposits seeds into the earth, he goes home and goes to sleep. Every morning he wakes up and doesn't see anything happening. Every night he goes back to sleep and he still can't see what's going on with the seeds. He can't see them growing and he doesn't have any idea how they grow, but they do. The soil manages to produce fruit all by itself!

"First comes the blade, then the sprig and finally, the full-grown stalk of wheat. As soon as the farmer sees that the fruit has arrived and that it is ripe for the picking, he goes out to harvest the crop before it's too late.

"God's community multiplies in the same mysterious and invisible way that seeds do. You can't see anything happening, but in due course, more and more people are transformed.

"What I want you to be clear about is this: when the soil is good, if a farmer plants seeds of wheat, he knows he'll end up with wheat; when he plants seeds of fruit, he knows he'll end up with fruit. So when you and I plant seeds of God's word in willing people's lives, the words will transform those people into children of God, who think and act like him. It is critical to pick the ripe fruit when it is ready, and not leave it out there until it's too late. You need to go out and bring people in while they are open and available, and not wait till they drop and are swallowed up in decay."

As I was talking, suddenly a man came running up to me and fell at my feet.

"Please, Sir, my little girl is sick in bed and not expected to make it through the day! She's my only daughter, and she's barely twelve years old! Please come and touch her, I beg you, so she can be healed and live!"

"Of course," I said at once, "Let's go!"

"Hurry!" said the panicked father, leading the way as we rushed towards his house. The locals told me that the man's name was Jairus and he was one of the leaders of the local congregation.

The crowds all followed me and my team members, making it difficult to move as quickly as Jairus wished. As we were trying to push our way through, someone came up behind me and touched my prayer shawl. I knew immediately that healing power had gone out of me, so I spun around and looked at the crowd.

"Who touched me?" I asked. "Who touched my clothes?"

"It wasn't me!" said one.

"Don't look at me!" said another, and they all denied touching me.

"How can you ask who touched you," said Peter, "when all these people are pushing and shoving others out of the way so they can be near you?"

"Somebody has touched me," I said, "because I sensed that great power just went out of me."

I took my time and looked through the crowd, searching for the one person that I knew had touched me. All of a sudden, a lady came forward and fell at my feet, trembling and crying in fear. She realized that she had been found out.

"I can't hide anymore," she said. "I'm the one who touched you! I have to tell the truth. I've been bleeding non-stop for twelve years now. I'm completely weakened from the loss of blood. I've gone to all kinds of doctors and spent all my money on all types of treatments trying to get better but nothing has worked. In fact, my condition has just kept going from bad to worse.

"My problem has affected my whole life. Everybody, including my family, has abandoned me because the law of God says that a woman who is bleeding is unclean. Nobody wants to come near me for fear of becoming contaminated. They all want to be pure so they can perform their religious rituals, but I am out here all alone!"

"I know," I said. "It says in the law of God that if a woman is bleeding, she must be kept away from others for seven days.

Anyone who touches her, or even sits down on a chair or bed that she has been on, is ritually unclean and has to wash from head to toe and wash his clothes and be considered unclean until evening. In addition, anyone who is sexually intimate with a bleeding woman will be unclean for seven days."[206]

"Yes," she said, her voice breaking. "My seven days have gone on for twelve whole years without letup! I've had to stay away from everyone, including my family. It's like being condemned to solitary for life. I feel so isolated. I'm sick and in quarantine. I can't have any friends. I have to live alone, eat alone, and sleep alone. I don't have anyone to talk to. I'm so lonely…

"But when I heard you were here," the lady was saying, "I decided to escape and go to you for help. I knew that even if I couldn't talk to you in person, if I could just touch your prayer shawl, I'd be healed. That's what I told myself, anyway, as I pushed my way through the crowd." The people in the crowd stepped back in disgust, wiping their hands on their clothes and hoping that they had not accidentally come in contact with the woman.

"When I finally saw you from behind, I pushed forward and came up behind you. As soon as I got close enough, I touched the healing tassels on the border of your prayer shawl, and instantly I felt the bleeding stop. I knew right away that I was healed! Now I want to tell you the truth publicly, in my defense, so you know why I touched you."

"Cheer up, sweet lady," I said. "Your faith has made you whole and delivered you from your illness. What you believed and acted on has healed you. Go in peace and enjoy your healthy body. You are now free!"

49

Dead Girl Skips Around the House

WHILE I WAS TALKING WITH the woman, we were interrupted by loud crying and wailing.

"It's too late, Jairus! Your daughter is dead!" screamed a group of relatives who had come running to tell Jairus the awful news. "Why bother Jesus any longer? She's gone!"

"Don't be afraid, Jairus," I said. "All you have to do is believe, and she will be made whole." Stunned, Jairus didn't know what to think, but he obeyed me and led us back to his house. His confused relatives hurried along behind us, wondering what was going on.

When we got there, I asked Peter, and the two sons of Zebedee, James and John, to accompany me inside. I told everyone else to stay outside. The four of us went into the house with Jairus. Once inside, we saw the commotion that was going on. People were crying and wailing loudly and the flute players were playing their sad funeral music.

"Why are you crying and carrying on like this?" I asked. "Go home please. Let me through to see the young girl. She's not dead. She's just asleep."

"You're crazy!" they mocked, laughing at me in disgust. "She's as dead as a doornail!" they said, because they knew she was gone.

"Please leave," I said. "All of you."

Jairus pushed all the people out of the house so we could be alone. I asked him and his wife to lead us to their daughter's bedroom. The little girl was laid out on the bed.

I went up to her, sat down on the bed, and took her by the hand.

"Talitha cumi!" I said, which means, "Young lady, I want you to get up now." As soon as I spoke those words, her spirit returned to her body and she awoke. She opened her eyes and immediately got up and skipped around the house feeling fine. Her parents were amazed beyond belief to see her alive again. They hugged her and kissed her, tears of joy running down their faces.

"Don't tell anyone what happened here," I told them. "And give her some food now. She must be hungry."

When the people saw that the little girl was alive, news of her miraculous resurrection back to life spread through the land. People started talking about the time when two of the greatest prophets had done the exact same thing centuries earlier.

The first was Elijah. There was a terrible famine in the land when God sent Elijah to a foreign widow on the Mediterranean coast, just a few miles south of Sidon. She gave him the very last bite of food she and her son had in the house. As a result, God blessed her and they never lacked food again.

However, one day the widow's son died. Elijah asked her for the boy's body. He carried him upstairs and laid him down on the bed. Then he cried out to God in prayer and the boy came back to life.[207]

Several years later, another prophet called Elisha was traveling, when a wonderful woman who was childless offered him hospitality. She and her husband even built a guest room onto their house so Elisha could stay there whenever he was in town. As a reward, Elisha blessed her and promised that she would have a son. God heard Elisha's prayer and the woman gave birth to a baby boy.

One day when he was older, the boy got a terrible headache and died in his mother's arms. She stretched him out on Elisha's bed and rushed out to get the prophet. Elisha went into the bedroom alone and prayed to God for the boy to live. God heard his prayer. The boy's spirit returned and he came back to life![208]

"Jesus must be a prophet!" the people said to one another. "He has brought a child back to life, just like Elijah and Elisha did! Could he indeed be the Savior we are looking for?"

50

Noisy Pair Get What They Want

WE LEFT JAIRUS' HOUSE AND headed back to our lodgings. Suddenly, I heard more loud screaming.

"Wait, Jesus! Stop! Please!"

I turned around and saw two blind men who were holding onto each other, feeling their way down the street, desperately trying to catch up with me.

"Descendant of King David! Please stop and take pity on us!" they yelled, running and stumbling all at the same time. "Stop! Please! We're blind! We can't see you!"

I went inside the house where I was staying, but they followed me right in.

"Do you really believe that I can heal you?" I asked them.

"Yes, Sir; we do," they both insisted. I touched their eyes and said:

"Receive whatever it is that you have believed." The eyes of both men were instantly healed and their vision was restored to normal. Obviously, they had believed.

They were so excited that even though I sternly warned them to keep the news of their healing to themselves and not tell anyone, they took off and spread the word about me all across the area. In fact, they came back and brought me a man who was mute and couldn't speak because he was demon-possessed.

I gave them their wish. I cast the demons out of the man and immediately he was able to speak. The crowds were amazed and openly admired me for the marvelous work I had done.

"This has never happened in Israel!" they said.

That's when some of the Spiritual Ones retaliated by saying, "He's only able to cast out demons by using the power of Satan, the ruler of the demons!" I didn't hesitate to correct them.

"Don't think for a minute that I've come to dismantle God's laws in the holy books, or the writings of the ancient prophets," I told them. "On the contrary, my mission is to make what they wrote about come true. I support God's laws one hundred percent. In fact, I want to clarify them for you so that you can see to what extent they impact your lives. I guarantee you that as long as the sky and the earth exist, every single letter, even the tiniest detail of God's law, will stand, until all prophecy in the holy books comes true.

"If you obey the commandments in God's law and teach others to follow your good example, you'll be called great and will be looked up to in his community. On the other hand, if you ever break God's law, or violate his principles, or ignore even one of the least important of his commandments,—or worse yet, teach other people to follow your bad example—you'll be considered the lowest in the community of God.

"What you need to realize is that your conduct has to be far superior to the good works you religious scholars and the Spiritual Ones currently do. You base your lives strictly on the external requirements of the religious law, without considering the spirit of love behind the law. If you continue to live like that, you don't have a hope of being a part of God's community."

"How can you possibly know what is in the holy books, when you have never studied them formally at the level of the legal experts?" said one of them arrogantly.

"My teachings aren't mine," I told them, "but they belong to the one who sent me. If you were willing to do what delights God, you would understand my teachings and know in your heart whether they are from God or whether I'm speaking of my own accord. People who speak their own words are usually looking for honor and recognition. But when people speak about God and want to give him glory, there is nothing wrong or unjust in that.

"Let me ask you a question. You say you are experts in religious law. Has knowing the law made any difference? Not really. You know the law but you don't keep the law. So who do you think you are, wanting to kill me for supposedly breaking the law? Isn't that a little bit of a double standard?"

"You're crazy with a demon!" they protested. "Who on earth is going around trying to kill you?"

"When I performed a miracle on the Day of Rest, you were all shocked!" I said, "You perform circumcision on baby boys on the eighth day, even if it falls on the Day or Rest, when you are not allowed to do any work. If you can do that procedure on the Day of Rest without being guilty of violating the religious law, why are you angry with me, when I restore a sick man to total health on the Day of Rest?

"Don't base your opinions on what you see. Base your decisions on what God expects; because he's the one who made the rules. You know that his law tells us that we should not judge out of partiality or fear of what people will think, but we are to be totally fair and do what is right."[209]

"The truth is that you each have enough to do just dealing with yourself, that you can't possibly have time to judge and criticize other people! Not unless you want to be judged and criticized yourself. Did you know that God will judge and sentence you to the same degree and with the same severity with which you dish out criticism and pass judgment on others? In fact, the scale you use to measure others' failings will be exactly the same scale God uses to measure all your mistakes!

"So ask yourself why you keep staring at others' imperfections, which are like little twigs in their eyes, when you yourself can't see your own major flaw, which, in comparison, is like a tree trunk sticking out of your own eye?

"How dare you say: 'Hold still a minute, so I can pull the little twig out of your eye!' while you're bumping into them with the tree trunk that is sticking out of your own eye? Please! You're acting like hypocrites! First take off your own mask of self-righteous perfection and remove the tree trunk out of your own eye. Then you'll be able to see clearly to pull the little twig out of other people's eyes.

"It's better not to judge and condemn others at all, because then you won't be judged and condemned either. In fact, instead of judging people, just forgive them and accept them for who they are; because if you forgive them, God will forgive you. So forgive, and you'll be forgiven.

"I suggest that you even take it a step further. Love them and be generous with them; because if you're generous with others, people will be so generous with you that you won't even be able to contain everything they give you!"

51

The Cure For Worry

AFTER THAT, I TOOK MY team members and we went back to my hometown of Nazareth. The following Day of Rest, I taught in our local assembly, where the members of the congregation had known me for most of my life. This time, they were ready to listen.

"I have something important to share with you today," I said. "It is impossible to serve two bosses at a time—or two gods, or two men, or two women, or even two goals!" I told them. "You can't be totally devoted to someone who deserves your absolute commitment, while at the same time be toying with someone else! You will always be comparing the two and feeling bitterness, anger and resentment towards one; and love and devotion to the other.

"What I'm saying is that you can't possibly give your entire devotion and service to both God and someone or something else at the same time, whether it's material possessions, worldly prestige, or any person or goal.

"If you choose to serve God, then be devoted to him, and him alone. You can't even be serving yourself at the same time as you're serving him. It just doesn't work that way. If you elect to serve him, then you can't give a single thought to your own life and your own well-being.

"If you choose to serve God, you can't waste your time worrying about your physical body. You can't worry about what you'll eat, what you'll drink, what kind of clothes you'll wear. Remember that the holy books instruct you to cast your burden on the Lord and he will take care of you!

"I know you're looking at me like this is impossible, but isn't life about more than just food, and the body about more than just clothes? Take a good look at birds, for example. Observe them carefully for a few weeks and you'll notice what simple lives they live. You'll never find them sowing seeds, or harvesting and storing food.

"They don't own any barns or storage sheds! Yet God feeds them all, just like the holy books say. He gives food to the animals and to the baby ravens that squawk in hunger.[210] That same God is your heavenly father. How much more valuable and more excellent are you than little birds?

"If you stop focusing on yourselves, you'll quit worrying about your physical needs. God looks after the sparrows, and you can buy five of them for only two little Roman coins. Just think how much more valuable you are! God is intimately aware of everything you need. He has even counted the number of hairs you have on you head. So stop worrying!"

"I have trouble trusting God like that," said an older woman. "I tend to worry a lot. What should I do?"

"You can't even make yourself grow a few inches taller just by worrying or willing yourself to grow, can you? Of course not! So if you're not able to do something as simple as controlling your height, why waste your energy worrying about your physical needs and desires? You act as if by focusing all your attention on them and worrying about them, you'll be able to change them!

"Let's take another example: clothes! Have you ever taken a good look at the wild lilies in the fields? If you observe wild lilies for several days, and carefully scrutinize how they grow, you'll never catch them working hard or manufacturing their own clothing. They don't exhaust themselves by spinning or sewing or knitting all day; but not even King Solomon, the wealthiest king who ever lived, was dressed as splendidly as one of these wild lilies!

"If God has designed wild flowers to be so beautiful, even though they are here today and gone tomorrow—wilted and dried up and tossed in the fire—don't you think he'll do an even better job of clothing you? You've never really believed or trusted God to take care of you because your faith is way too small!

"But I challenge you to stop worrying about yourselves, and stop worrying about your future. Stop saying, 'But what are we going to eat and drink? How are we going to buy clothes?' You keep yourselves in a constant state of unnecessary upset. People all around the world worry about all these things. They are always stressed out and worried about how they will meet their own needs, but they're looking for solutions in all the wrong places!

"You should act differently," I told the woman, and everyone else in the assembly hall. "You have a heavenly father who feeds the birds and clothes the lilies. Don't you realize that he understands perfectly well that you need and want all the same things that unbelievers do? So let him take care of you; and you, in turn, take care of establishing his everlasting community here on Earth. Just focus on doing his will and helping others change their hearts and return to him. If you do that, all these other material things will be provided for you."

"Stop being little spiritual babies, terrified and running away from God like frightened sheep! God is eager to freely give you his supernatural kind of life. Not only is he standing by to give it to you, he's very willing and determined to make it happen. In fact, helping you live his kind of life gives him great pleasure!

"So stop being anxious and worried about tomorrow. Tomorrow will bring with it a whole new set of problems and worries! Today, you already have plenty to do handling your old ways of thinking and current evil habits of the mind, as well as all the things you're already fussing and worrying about. You really don't have time to bog yourself down with the future and any potential problems it may hold!"

Many in the audience were amazed at the depth of my understanding.

"Where does this man get such incredible wisdom from?" they whispered to each other. "We've heard that he's performing all kinds of miracles! But isn't he a carpenter? Isn't he the son of Joseph, our local carpenter here? Isn't his mother named Mary? Aren't James, Joseph, Judas and Simon his brothers? Aren't these girls that are here with us his sisters? So where does he get all this wisdom from?"

Once again, the people of my home town were offended by my boldness; but I wasn't surprised.

"Any prophet who knows God intimately" I said, "and is able to communicate his secrets to others is honored, respected and appreciated everywhere—except in his own hometown, and by his own family."

Although I was able to touch a few people and heal them, I wasn't able to do any great miracles or wonders in Nazareth because of their unbelief. On the contrary, I was amazed and disappointed at my neighbors' lack of faith. They obviously didn't trust in the God of promise! But I wasn't the first to be disappointed in people's lack of faith and recognition of God's hand. The prophet Jeremiah also realized that in his day there was nobody with faith, and there was nobody to pray to God on behalf of the people.

"There's not much I can do here in Nazareth," I told my group. "Let's move on."

52

Briefing For Critical Mission

WE LEFT NAZARETH AGAIN AND walked in a circuit through all the surrounding towns and villages. Galilee was a fertile agricultural area, and everywhere we went we saw farmers tending to their crops and their olive trees. It was also a very cosmopolitan trading area. As we walked along, we ran into merchants on their way to Egypt, or the Mediterranean, or the Far East. We talked to other travelers along the way, many of whom had immigrated to the area and intermarried with the local Hebrews, giving the area the name of Galilee of the Nations.[211]

I stopped to teach in each of the Hebrew congregations in the area. At every meeting I told them the good news and invited them to be a part of God's community. At the same time, I healed every sickness and every disease of all the people they brought to me.

As I saw the multitudes of people in need everywhere, I was touched to the core by their helplessness. They were exhausted, like sheep, scattered without a shepherd. They reminded me of the days when Moses crossed the desert with the Hebrew people, because he described them as sheep without a shepherd.[212]

Several of the ancient prophets had also referred to the people of their day as lost sheep, scattered all around the world. They were all lost, each doing his own thing.[213] Nobody bothered to go looking for them, except God, who searches for lost people, just like a shepherd looks for his lost sheep, to bring them back into the fold.[214]

I was so impacted by the people's needs that I called a special meeting of my twelve representatives. I had them stand together in pairs. Simon Peter with his brother Andrew; James, the son of Zebedee with his brother John; Philip with Bartholomew; Thomas with Matthew the tax collector; James the son of Alphaeus with Thaddeus; and finally Simon from Canaan with Judas Iscariot, who would eventually betray me.

"Brothers," I said, as they stood there, two by two, looking at me intently, "we're facing a critical situation. The people who need to be brought into God's spiritual community are like a huge harvest ready to be gathered into the barn, but there aren't enough harvesters to get the job done! I want you to pray to God and specifically ask him to send workers out to look for people and bring them into God's spiritual community.

"It's time now for you to go out and put into practice what I've been teaching you. It's time for you to go out and help people," I said.

"Today I'm going to give you your final instructions. When I finish, you'll be heading out in pairs and working together as partners. I'm giving you executive powers over evil spirits and the authority to cast them out of people. I'm also giving you the power and authority to heal every kind of sickness, disease and sexual problem! Right after we finish this briefing, you'll be on your way. So listen carefully, because I'm going to give you specific orders for your trip!" I said.

I paused to look at the men. They were all standing at attention and listening intently. They knew their lives depended on what I was saying.

"I don't want you going into any areas where foreigners live at this time," I instructed them. "Don't go to any Samaritan towns either, because they are only half-Hebrew. Right now, I only want you to focus on the lost sheep of the house of Israel—look only for Hebrews who are racially pure.

"As you go, tell them the good news. Tell them that God's spiritual community can be accessed now and that it's here, just a breath away. Use the power that I've given you to miraculously heal the sick. Pick up those without strength, dignity or authority and give them hope again. Find the weak and powerless and put them back on their feet.

"Look for the lonely outcasts suffering from leprosy and heal them and set them free from the disgrace of their disease. Go find the bodies of those who've died of natural causes and raise them back to life. Go free possessed people from the demonic spirits that control them!"

As I spoke, I could see courage and enthusiasm welling up in my team members. They had been preparing for this day and they were eager to set off on their own and try out what I had taught them.

"You have received all of God's blessings and power," I explained, "and you never had to pay for them, did you? So don't charge others for them either. Be generous and freely give people what they need because you've received what you need without having to pay for it."

I ordered them not to take anything with them for the trip, except a walking stick.

"Don't even take any money with you. Don't put any copper, gold, silver or brass coins in your money belts. Don't take any travel bags. Don't even take a sack lunch or a beggar's bag 'just in case'! Wear comfortable walking shoes and only take the clothes on your back. Don't take an extra coat, shoes, shirt,—or even a spare walking stick.

"I believe that if you work for God, you should be fed and taken care of financially by our people. As you know, we Hebrews are used to feeding the Levite priests, who serve God and own no land. Down through the ages, even kings have given gifts to God's priests and prophets. I'm sure you remember how our very first king, King Saul, felt it was an honor to give to the man of God. That tradition of hospitality to God's servants has continued on down through the ages, and that is what you will encounter also.[215]

"Whenever you arrive in a new Hebrew town or city, ask around and find out which family deserves to receive you in their home. Then go find that family. When you arrive on their doorstep, introduce yourselves and tell them why you are there. If they do in fact deserve to have you stay with them, they will respond eagerly by welcoming you into their home. Accept their hospitality! Go inside and stay with them the whole time you are in town, leaving only when it's time to move on, and share the peace that you have in your hearts with that household.

"But if you're standing on the doorstep and a Hebrew man or woman refuses to welcome you in, or sends you away, or even criticizes or persecutes you, not wanting to listen to what you have to say, that family obviously doesn't deserve the blessing of your company. Don't let them upset you. Don't get frustrated.

"Just stay calm and walk away. As you leave the house and exit the city gates, symbolically shake the dust off your feet as a sign of judgment against them. As you do, your peace will come back to you. Trust me, when Judgment Day arrives, it will be more tolerable for the wicked people of Sodom and Gomorrah than for the people of any city that turns its back on you.

53

Doves, Sheep And Snakes

"BE AS HARMLESS AS DOVES," I said, smiling. "Doves only fly in and land where the surroundings are peaceful. They are symbols of innocence and they never cause any harm. So be honest and sincere; be openly vulnerable with people. Don't have a hidden agenda and don't trick or deceive anybody by saying things that aren't true.

"At the same time," I warned them sternly, "know that it's dangerous out there! I'm sending you out like helpless little sheep into a pack of starving wolves. Sheep are vulnerable. They are not equipped to defend themselves—no fangs, no claws, no loud bark, no venom, no offensive spray. Sheep can't even run fast enough to escape! Their only protection is their shepherd. They are designed to live in a close relationship with their shepherd for their very survival.

"You can't just trust everyone. Some people are dangerous. So be careful!" I urged them. "Use your common sense and be as smart as snakes. Snakes are symbols of caution and wisdom. They know how to escape danger and slither away quickly and skillfully. You need to be alert and avoid danger whenever possible.

"Don't look so shocked! I'm telling you that there are people out there who will want to arrest you and drag you in front of their city councils—and some will succeed! They will even beat you publicly in their religious assemblies! They will force you to appear before governors and kings just because you follow me. But be thankful, because you will be able to be a witness for me to both Hebrews and foreigners alike.

"When they turn you over to the authorities," I instructed them, "don't worry about what you're going to say. When the time comes for you to respond to their questioning, God will give you the appropriate response. You will not have to think of a single word! The spirit of God, your father, who speaks in you, will speak through you and give you all the words you need in that moment.

"Remember King David?" I asked them. "The spirit of God spoke through him and God's words were on his tongue.[216] Remember when God called Moses, and Moses was afraid to speak in public? God told him to go anyway, and he would teach him what to say.[217]

"Remember the prophet Jeremiah? He told God that he couldn't preach because he was just a kid; but God told him not to talk like that, because he would give him the words he needed when he needed them.[218] So don't worry. God will be with you and give you the guidance and inspiration that you need, right when you need it!

"Realize, however, that following me has its price," I said, looking them each in the eye. What I had to say next was very serious.

"Some of you have brothers and sisters who will turn you in to the authorities for going against their religion."

The men gasped.

"Oh, yes. They will say that you have disrespected God and should be killed for blasphemy, just like they have said about me! Remember—as students, you are not greater than your teacher; as employees, you are not greater than your boss. If they have called me, the head of God's household, 'Beelzebub' and 'Satan', be prepared for them to say much worse things about you! Expect it, because there is no reason why you would be treated better than your teacher or your boss!" I said.

"Worse yet," I warned them, "some of you have parents who will betray you; and some of you have children who will turn on you and arrange for your capture. They will call you religious deserters and insist that you get the death penalty!"

My closest friends, my brothers, were listening carefully to the seriousness of my words.

"This is nothing new," I explained. "Remember how the prophet Micah wrote that family members would turn on each other—and that a man's enemies would be living in his very own house?[219] The men looked sad. They remembered exactly the scripture I was referring to.

"People who hate me," I said, "are automatically going to hate you—just because you are acting as my substitute and my representative in their lives. When they realize that you are my followers, some will be prejudiced against you without even knowing you. Don't kid yourselves; it won't be easy.

"But if you continue in the faith despite all the problems that are thrown at you, including suffering and persecution, and you do it with patience and faith to the very end, you will eventually be delivered from danger and suffering.

"But be smart. When you see that people are persecuting you in one town, quickly escape and go on to the next one. I promise you that you will not have completed the rounds of all the Hebrew towns and villages before I return.

"That's why I'm giving you fair warning and telling you exactly what to expect. Don't be afraid of them. Publicly declare to them what I have told you in private. Boldly proclaim what I whisper in your ear to the people I send you to. Shout it from the housetops, because it's time for everything that is hidden from view to be exposed, and everything that is secret to be revealed.

"So don't be afraid of people. They only have the power to kill your body, but they can't touch your soul! When given a choice between fearing people and fearing God, it's better to be afraid of God, because he is able to destroy both your body and your soul in hell!" I said.

"Don't be scared of what other people are afraid of," I said. "Instead, remember that God is above everyone and everything. You should be afraid only of God; you should be terrified of displeasing him,[220] because if you respect and obey God, he will be a safe hiding place for you!

"You know that down at the market little sparrows are very cheap, don't you?" I continued. "Well, not even one of those little birds will fall to the ground without God, your father, knowing. If God knows the exact number of hairs in your head at any given moment, do you think that anything can happen to you without him knowing? So don't be afraid. Aren't you a lot more valuable than a whole flock of sparrows?

"Remember that the people out there are sinful and their ways are opposed to God. But God is watching everything, and

I'm standing with you. If you publicly acknowledge me in front of people, even when you're afraid, I will publicly acknowledge you in front of my father who is in heaven. But if you deny knowing me to other people, I will also deny knowing you before my father.

"Don't think for a minute that my coming to the world will bring peace and rest and make everybody happy and get along! I haven't come to bring peace, but a sword! Because of me, men will turn on their own fathers; daughters will turn on their mothers; and daughters-in-law will turn on their mothers-in-law! Your enemies will turn out to be your own relatives!

"King David understood that kind of betrayal. He was betrayed by his close friend. If it had been an enemy, he could have stood it; but it was his trusted friend who wanted him dead![221]

"I'm warning you, if you live for the common goals and interests you have with your mother or father rather than following me, you don't deserve to follow me. If you live for the common goals and interests you have with your son or daughter rather than being with me, you don't deserve to be with me!

"Everyone who is condemned to death by crucifixion has to carry his own cross to the crucifixion site. Realize up front that following me could lead to your death. If you refuse to pick up your cross, deny yourself and follow me, you don't deserve to follow me. If you make a life for yourself and selfishly cling to it, you'll actually end up losing it. But if you let go of your own life for my sake, and live instead for God and his goals and interests, then you will find real life.

"When you make following me your priority, every time you meet new people and they welcome you, know that they are welcoming me; and by welcoming me, they are opening their lives up to God, who sent me. What's more, if they welcome you and treat you as a prophet and a servant of God, you will be able to give them the type of reward only a prophet can give.

"Remember how the foreign widow fed the prophet Elijah her last bit of food during a terrible famine? Well, Elijah blessed her and she never ran out of food during the long famine that devastated her neighbors. More importantly, when her only son became ill and died, Elijah prayed to God and God brought the boy back to life! Those were incredible blessings that she would never have received had she not opened her home to Elijah, despite her great poverty.

"Remember the wealthy woman from Shunem who built an addition onto her house just for the prophet Elisha? As a reward, Elisha prayed that the woman would have a son, and years later, when the son died, Elisha prayed and brought him back to life! She would never have received this miracle had she not first blessed the prophet.

"When you arrive at someone's house and they treat you with the respect due to a person who has dedicated his life to God, you will be able to bless them in ways that only a person of faith can. Even if they give you something as basic as a glass of water to drink, I promise you that they will be rewarded for their kindness and generosity."

I finished briefing my new partners for their exploratory journey and they took off in pairs for the surrounding areas. Everywhere they went, they engaged everyone they ran across in conversation about their spiritual lives.

"Look back over your past," they urged people. "Examine your lives, and if you have any failures and regrets, make the decision to go forward into the future with a new attitude. Learn from your past mistakes and be wiser for your failures."

My team members had no trouble casting out demons and evil spirits wherever people wanted to be set free from severe physical and mental suffering. They were also able to ritually rub healing oil on those that were sick and without strength, and heal them by faith on my authority. While they were out busily using their delegated skills, I went on to teach in other villages.

54

The Birthday Party

MEANWHILE, BACK IN Governor Herod's palace high up in Fort Machaerus, his new wife Herodias was still busy plotting to get rid of my cousin John. She was tired of him sitting in prison at the fortress and continuing to preach against her adulterous marriage.

"Our private life is none of John's business!" she kept telling her husband. "He's turned our marriage into a public mockery. I want him silenced forever. Come on, Dear. Do it for me. Don't you want to make me happy?"

Herodias hated that nagging feeling of unease. With John out of the way, she would be able to flaunt her new relationship without guilt.

"I don't want to kill the man," her husband would say. "He's too popular! Besides, I like his teachings."

"You can't afford to keep him alive, Honey," she would tell her husband as often as he would listen. "Remember what trouble your father went to when he had all those babies in Bethlehem killed? John wants everyone to believe that a royal baby slipped through your father's fingers and is still alive!

"Now John is promoting this Jesus and telling people that he is the long-awaited Hebrew king! That's an insult to your father!

If what John says is true, and there is a 'king' who escaped your father's baby massacre—you're in for big trouble! The sooner John is gone, the sooner this movement can be put down."

Still, the Governor was not ready to act; but his wife refused to give up. One day, the perfect occasion presented itself for Herodias to make her move. Herod's birthday was coming and he was planning a huge birthday celebration. He invited all his lords, his high-ranking military men, and the wealthy landowners of Galilee to a royal banquet at his fortress palace.

The big day came and guests arrived from far and wide to recline on cushions and eat the delicious food. The wine flowed freely, and as the party heated up, Herod called for his beautiful teenage step-daughter, Salome.

"Dance for us, Baby!" he said.

The musicians started to play, and his guests settled back to watch the performance. Salome mesmerized the audience. She danced feverishly to the beat of the music, her arms and body exploding with energy. She was a total sensation. Everyone clapped and cheered and wanted more.

"That was a beautiful performance, Sugar," said the delighted Herod spontaneously in front of all his guests. "Ask me for anything, and I'll give it to you! I swear, I'll give you anything you want—even half my kingdom!"

"Thank you, my lord," Salome bowed politely. The guests broke out in cheers and claps yet again. Salome ran proudly to her mother for a congratulatory hug.

"He told me I could have anything I want, Mother," she said excitedly. "He said I danced beautifully and he wants to reward me publicly. What should I ask for?"

The Birthday Party

Herodias didn't hesitate:

"Ask him for the head of John the Baptist, Honey!" she replied. "Go! Quick, before he changes his mind!" Salome hurried back to make her request. Herod stood up and raised his hand, calling for all the guests to listen.

"So what can I give you, my Precious?" he cooed.

"I want you to give me the head of John the Baptist on a big serving dish right now!" she said.

Everyone gasped in shock. Governor Herod Antipas was stunned. The color drained from his face. Suddenly he felt sick to his stomach and deeply regretted his impulsive words. But he had made the promise to Salome in front of all his guests; he could not back down now! He didn't want to lose face and he didn't want to totally humiliate his new step-daughter and cause even more problems with his new wife.

"Whatever you wish, my Darling," said Herod to Salome. "Executioner—you heard the request! Go immediately and do what she has asked! Get John's head on a platter right away!"

The executioner didn't have far to go. He went straight to John's cell and beheaded him at once. Then he brought his head back on a platter and handed it to Salome, who carried it off to her mother.

A delegation of John's followers arrived in Galilee to give me the shocking news.

"Your cousin John is dead, Teacher!" they wailed. "His life has been tragically cut short. Herod finally got him! Your cousin was executed at Herod's birthday party banquet. We rushed over as soon as we heard. Herodias insisted on keeping John's head, but we were able to get his body back. We carried him, headless, back home to his family in Hebron. They buried him just a few days ago!"

Uncle Zach and Aunt Beth's miracle baby was dead! My heart broke. Losing my cousin in such a horrific manner was terrible. Once again, one of the greatest prophets of all time had gone to his untimely grave.

Meanwhile, the Governor was more agitated than ever. As word reached him that I was alive and well and performing miracles, he panicked.

"People say that Jesus of Nazareth is John the Baptist come back to life!" he reported to his closest advisors. "That's why he's doing all these miracles!"

"We've heard that he's Elijah come back to earth," they replied. "But then other people say that he is a prophet, or at least like one of the great prophets."

"You're wrong!" the Governor insisted. He was starting to get paranoid, just like his father, Herod the Great had been, when I was a baby in Bethlehem. "He must be John the Baptist come back to life! I know it! Who else could he be? I beheaded John and now he's come back to life again to haunt me!" he cried. "I want to meet Jesus in person and see for myself who he really is!"

55

A Boy's Sack Lunch Feeds Thousands

WITH MY COUSIN JOHN DEAD, I was all the more determined to keep spreading the good news. I gathered my team of twelve representatives and sent them out again into the villages nearby to preach and to heal. When they returned from their mission, they were excited to share everything that had happened on the trip, but we couldn't really talk. We were constantly surrounded by people, and interrupted by their comings and goings. We had no privacy. We didn't even have time to eat.

"Come away with me for a while," I said. "I want to spend some quality time alone with you so you can tell me all about your trip. There's a remote retreat not too far from Capernaum. It's on the northeast shore, outside the fishing village of Bethsaida. It'll be a great place for you to take a break and rest."

We slipped out and sailed privately by boat across Lake Galilee, hoping nobody would see us; but some of the people spotted us leaving and recognized me. Word quickly spread and folks from all the little towns rushed along the shore. They figured out that we were heading for Bethsaida and some of them managed to outrun the boat. They were already waiting on the shore when we pulled in to land.

I climbed out of the boat and looked at all the people that had run, yes, run to meet me. I was so moved. They really were like sheep without a shepherd. Obviously we were not going to have a private retreat after all! Hundreds more were right behind them, eager to get close to me.

"Come join us," I said. "I came here to get away with my followers, but you are thirsty to hear. Come be with us!" Those who had outrun the boat followed us up a small hill. I sat down with my team members. Many more soon arrived. Some were sick and needed healing, so I healed them. Then I spent the afternoon teaching.

"How can you tell if you're living God's way?" I asked. They sat, deep in thought, but nobody answered.

"Have you ever looked into the eyes of a dead person?" I continued. "They just have a blank stare. Now look at each other's eyes. They're full of life! So it's the eyes that light up a person's body, giving it life and animation.

"If the look in your eyes is clear and honest, your whole life is full of brightness and light. Then you are full of light, just like when you light a candle and the brightness of its flame gives you total light and clear visibility.

"But if the look in your eyes is shifty, evasive or evil, your whole life is full of darkness and unhappiness, forcing everything to stop, and bringing everything to a standstill. That kind of darkness is very deep! So look inside yourselves and carefully examine your motives. Make very sure that what is in you is not darkness, error, ignorance, misery and eternal damnation."

After I had been teaching and healing for a long while, Philip interrupted me.

"Excuse me, Sir," he said, "it's getting very late and we're out here in the middle of nowhere! Don't you think it's time

A Boy's Sack Lunch Feeds Thousands

to dismiss the crowds? They've been here for hours without food. Shouldn't we send them on their way before it gets dark so they can go look for food and lodging in the nearby villages?"

"No, Philip," I said, "they don't need to go anywhere! You give them something to eat! Where can we buy enough food to feed all these people?" I specifically asked Philip this to test him and show him how unbelieving he was, because I already knew what he would say.

"You want us to go to the nearest store and buy food and give it to them?" he argued with me. "There are about five thousand men here, not to mention women and children! We only have about two hundred coins in the treasury. That's nowhere near enough to feed all these people!"

Philip was reacting just like Moses, who snapped at God and asked where he was supposed to get food in the middle of the desert for a whole nation![222] On a similar occasion, a servant protested when his master, the prophet Elisha, instructed him to feed a hundred men with twenty loaves of bread and some cornhusks! But God promised that there would be enough for all, with food left over! So Elisha's servant set out what they had, and sure enough, the hundred men all ate till they were satisfied; and there was still food left over![223]

"Go and find out how many loaves of bread you have," I said. My team members mingled with the crowd and Andrew came back with the answer.

"We found a boy who has five loaves of barley bread and two small fish, but that's nothing when we have so many mouths to feed!"

"Andrew—you go get the boy's loaves and fishes," I said, ignoring his skepticism. "In the meantime, I need the rest of you to organize everyone into groups." So they started to sit the people down on the green grass in clusters of fifty and a hundred. When Andrew came back with the five loaves and two fish, I looked up to heaven and spoke a blessing over the food. I picked up the loaves and broke them into pieces. Then I took a pocket knife and cut the fish into segments.

"Here," I said, "take these and serve the people so they can start eating."

They carried the food from group to group all over the hillside, serving everyone as much as they wanted, and miraculously, there was enough food for all. When the people had finished eating, I called my team members over.

"Take some baskets and go back around to pick up all the leftovers so that nothing is wasted," I said. They took off and picked up twelve basketfuls of leftovers.

"This is incredible!" said a man in the audience when he saw how I had miraculously fed everyone. "You must be the Great Prophet that we're expecting to come back to earth! Nobody since the prophet Elisha has done anything like this! You might even be the Peaceful One, who will come and gather people of all races together!

"What happened here is just like what happened to our ancestors when they left slavery in Egypt and walked through the desert for forty years with no means of support and no food, and God fed several million people with a honey-bread called manna! Here we all are, with nothing to eat but five loaves of

A Boy's Sack Lunch Feeds Thousands

bread and two fish, and you end up feeding over five thousand people! That's incredible!"

As I watched the people's reaction, I realized that sooner or later, they would come and get me and try to force me to be their king, so they could keep getting free food. Of course, I would not let that happen. I had made that very clear to Satan back in my desert boot camp. As soon as my team had finished picking up all the leftovers, I immediately ordered them to get into the boat and sail back to Capernaum on the opposite side of the lake from Bethsaida. I stayed behind to dismiss the crowds.

Once the last ones were safely on their way, I slipped away privately and went up into a mountain to pray. Passover was almost upon us. It was definitely time for me to get away. I decided to spend that night alone up in the mountains.

56

Believer Walks On Water!

BY EVENING, THE BOAT CARRYING my team back to Capernaum was in the middle of the lake and I was still up in the hills alone, praying. As night fell, a strong wind developed, causing the lake waters to swell. Powerful waves started to batter the boat. From the hilltop high above them, I could see that they were really struggling in the rough waves. They were pulling as hard as they could on the oars, but were making little progress because of the strong winds.

They did the best they could, all through the night. At about five in the morning I walked out on the water to catch up with them.[224] By this point, they had rowed really far out on the lake. When they looked back and saw me walking on the surface of the water and getting closer to their boat, they screamed out in fear, thinking that I was a ghost. They were terrified out of their minds, thinking that death was near.

"Cheer up, friends! It's me!" I waved. "Don't be afraid." When I got close to the boat, I walked on past them, acting as if I was going to walk all the way to Capernaum on the waves and not stop.

Peter was the first to react.

"Sir," he called out, "Wait! If it's really you, order me to walk on the water and come over to you!"

Believer Walks On Water!

"Come on then," I said.

So Peter climbed out of the boat. He put his feet down on top of the waves and started walking on the surface of the lake towards me. Everyone was amazed. But after the initial rush of faith, Peter took his eyes off me and started worrying about the strong winds blowing the waves at him. Then he looked down at the rough water below his feet. That's when fear got hold of him! His feet started to sink and he lost his balance.

"Help me, Teacher! Help!" he screamed out in panic.

I reached out and grabbed his arm to steady him, so he could keep on walking.

"You don't have much faith, do you, Peter?" I said. "You have just enough to start the job, but then you begin to doubt. Why?"

The others watched as we walked together towards the boat and climbed back in. Everyone eagerly clustered around me to welcome me aboard. Then the winds died down, as if worn out by the storm.

My team members had been unmoved by the miracle of the bread and fish; but now that they had been in personal danger and they really needed my help, all of a sudden the things that I could do for them became extremely important.

"You really are the Son of God!" they said, filled with wonder at what had happened. When they saw how Peter had walked on the water, and how I had calmed the waves, they were amazed. They went back to rowing and, after an uneventful trip, our boat arrived at Capernaum harbor.

57

Two Kinds of Food

WHEN WE REACHED CAPERNAUM, we rowed the boat closer to shore and dropped anchor in Gennesaret, a fertile area of about three miles, where they grew figs, olives, palms and walnut trees. As soon as we got out of the boat, the local people recognized me.

Word spread like wildfire that I was back. People ran throughout the region and brought everyone who was ill to see me, even if they had to carry them in on mats and stretchers. They had heard that everywhere I went, whether it was a village, a town, a rural home or marketplace, people laid their sick down along the streets in front of me.

The people of Capernaum begged me to at least allow them to touch the edge of my prayer shawl, because they believed I would heal them; and in fact, every single sick person who touched me was healed and became perfectly well.

Meanwhile, back in Bethsaida, some of the people who had eaten at the miraculous feeding of the five thousand woke up the following morning to find only one boat left and my team members gone. While they were speculating where I could be, several fancy boats arrived from King Herod's capital, Tiberias. They were full of tourists who had heard that I had fed the multitudes free food and they wanted to check it out for themselves.

Two Kinds of Food

They joined in the search for me but it soon became clear that I wasn't there. They decided to pile back into the boats and sail to Capernaum to see if I was there. When they found me, they came rushing up to me.

"Sir," they said, flustered, "why did you take off and come all the way here?"

"I'm going to tell you something you may not like to hear," I said. "You've come looking for me, not because you saw my healing miracles, but because you ate the free food that I gave you and your stomachs were filled.

"But here's the problem: food eventually spoils and becomes worthless. So don't waste your time and energy working for food to feed your physical bodies. Instead, devote your time to working for the heavenly food that produces spiritual life, because that lasts forever. If you follow me, I will give you that spiritual food. In fact, God specifically sent me here to give it to you."

"So tell us, once and for all," the tourists demanded, "What is the heavenly food that produces spiritual life? How should we spend our time if we want to devote ourselves to doing God's work?"

"The answer is very simple," I said. "This is what you should do: believe in me, because God has sent me to you. Get to know me, understand my teachings, and trust me enough to put my words into practice."

"All right," they argued, "so what sign or miracle are you going to show us to prove that you have supernatural powers, or that you are connected to God in some way, so that we can have proof and believe in you? Moses gave our ancestors the miraculous manna bread from heaven for forty years in the desert. It was proof of his power. They gathered the grain daily, so they could grind it up and bake it and boil it. What are you going to do to prove yourself?"

I could tell that they hadn't heard a word of what I had just said.

"Let me tell you something," I answered. "In the first place, the bread was called 'manna', which means 'what is it?' because they had no idea how it got there. In the second place, it wasn't Moses who gave them the manna bread from heaven. It was God himself; because God has true heavenly food, and he wants to give it to you as well."

I paused.

"I am that true heavenly food, the real bread from God. I am like living bread from God. It's not that I'm physical food. It's that I come to you fresh, daily, to meet all your needs. I have come from heaven to bring spiritual life to this beautiful world and all the people in it."

"We'd love to eat a bread that brings spiritual life! That's exactly what we want, Sir," they shouted. "Give it to us forever!"

"I am that bread of life, the bread of God's presence. If you come to me, you'll never again have to slave away for your daily bread or starve with hunger. And if you believe in me, you'll never again be thirsty. But here's the problem: you keep listening to what I'm telling you and observing all the miracles that I do, but you still don't believe me." They looked at me as if I had more to say, but I ended my teaching and left.

The following Day of Rest, I was back speaking in the new assembly hall at Capernaum.

Two Kinds of Food

"Every person that God has given to me naturally wants to get close to me; and if you are one of those people, and you reach out to me, there's no way that I'll ever turn you away or throw you out! I would not do that even if I wanted to, because I didn't come to earth to do whatever I please. No. I came down from heaven to do what God wants me to do, because he's the one who sent me here."

"What does God want you to do?" an elderly man asked.

"It's very specific," I replied. "Let me tell you exactly what he wants me to do; he wants me to keep you safe. He doesn't want me to lose a single one of you that he has given to me.

"Here's what else he wants me to do: he wants me to give every one of you who trust in me a spiritual life that is constant and never-ending. In other words, he wants you to live forever. Once you experience that moment-by-moment spiritual life, when the last day comes—the Day of Final Judgment, I will raise you all up to heaven, even if you are already dead by then!"

They looked at me, puzzled and shocked by what I was saying.

"I am the real bread of life," I declared. "Our ancestors ate the manna in the wilderness, but they are all dead now. I'm the manna that comes down from heaven so that you can eat of me daily and never die. I am like living bread—warm and nutritious. If you eat of me you'll live forever. My human body is like bread which I give as a gift to the world, so that everyone will have an opportunity to live a vibrant spiritual life."

The people in the congregation were getting angry.

"How can you give us your flesh to eat? That's ridiculous!" said one of the leaders.

"Let me tell you something," I said. "I am your humble servant and if you don't eat my flesh and drink my blood, you will not have this spiritual life in you. But if you do eat of me, you'll have God's eternal life in you and I will raise you up on the last day. My flesh is real food and my blood is real drink. If you eat my flesh and drink my blood, you'll remain alive and you'll stand firm in me and I in you, because my flesh is the presence of God, and my blood is the life of God."

The people looked visibly distressed. They didn't like me saying that I was the bread of life that comes down from heaven.

"God the father has sent me here and I live because of him," I continued. "In the same way, if you eat me, you'll keep on living a vibrant, spiritual life, day after day, now and into eternity!"

"Isn't he the carpenter's son?" the whisper went through the congregation again. "How can he say that he's come down from heaven, when we know he's the son of Mary and Joseph from Nazareth?"

"Stop gossiping and complaining!" I said, knowing what they were thinking. "You can't possibly come to me unless God first draws you to me by his love; and God won't stop until you are at a point where you can choose for yourselves whether you want to respond to him or not. God never gives up. He loves you and he won't stop pursuing you until he has won your hearts![225]

"The prophet Jeremiah wrote that God promises to put his law and his teachings deep inside you—in your heart, your thoughts, your conscience, and in your innermost feelings. He will put his direction and instructions in your entire being. He will be your God, and you will be his people," I explained.

"You will not have to teach one another anymore. An ox is

Two Kinds of Food

trained using a yoke. A horse is trained using reins, a bit between his teeth and the sharp-toothed wheels on the spurs. Humans are trained using the Law of God.

"But once God's Law is in your hearts, you will no longer have to persuade your friends and family to get to know God. You will not need religious ritual and fear of punishment to force them to behave, because they will all know God, from the least important to the greatest.

"Remember how the prophet Isaiah wrote that all your children will be taught by God, and their peace will be great?" I asked them.[226] "Remember how the prophet Micah wrote that God promised to pour out words like rain and teach you his ways, which are the paths of life and death?"[227]

"If you hear my father's instructions and learn from him and put his words into practice, you'll naturally want to be with me. God will forgive all your sins and forget all your wrongdoings! He forgives and forgets. Isn't that wonderful?" I said.

"Nobody has ever seen God, except for me, and I'm here to tell you that if you believe in me, you already have everlasting life and I will raise you up in the Day of Judgment."

After listening to me teach in the congregation in Capernaum, many of my closest followers finally understood what I was saying and they complained to each other privately.

"What he's saying is really tough!" they murmured. "Who can stand to listen to him? Who can even understand him? Who can actually do what he's saying?" they grumbled. I could tell that they were disgusted.

"My words offend you, don't they?" I said. "My words are spiritual life. It's the spirit that brings the dead to life. Now imagine your reaction if you actually saw me going back up to heaven!

"But it really doesn't matter what I say," I explained. "Some of you just won't believe me, no matter what. That's why I told you that you can't come to me without God first drawing you to him and giving you that desire."

My inner circle of twelve had grown to a large number of close followers by this time; but after this conversation, many of them decided to quit and go back home. Following me was too much for them. They found it too confrontational; too uncomfortable; too costly.

"Will you also leave me and go back home?" I asked my twelve personally chosen representatives.

"Sir, who else can we turn to?" said Peter, always the first to blurt something out. "You have the powerful words of constant and everlasting life. We believe you and we're sure that you're the holy one that our people have been expecting for centuries."

"You're right, Peter. And haven't I personally selected the twelve of you, even knowing full well that one of you is a devil?" I asked. I was referring to Judas Iscariot, because even though he was one of my original twelve representatives, it was he who was destined to betray me. They weren't really sure what I meant by one of them being a devil, so nobody said a word after that. They just stayed really quiet, thinking about the cost of following me.

58

Clean Body Or Pure Heart?

OUR PEOPLE WERE ALWAYS WASHING. They went to the men's or women's public baths like the Greeks and Romans did. They washed the dust from their feet whenever they walked inside a house. They washed different parts of their body, including their hands, many times a day.

Whenever they came home from the market, for example, they wouldn't touch any food without first washing their hands; and they always washed their hands before eating.

They also performed ceremonial washing for religious reasons. According to the holy books, they became contaminated by childbirth, menstruation, contact with a corpse or a disease, such as leprosy, and sexual contact. That's when they had to purify themselves by bathing and washing their clothes, their cups, pots, brass bowls and the linens that covered the couches on which they reclined during meals.

A member of the Spiritual Ones came up to me one day and begged me to come and eat with him and his friends. When I entered his house, I sat down without first going through the customary hand-washing ceremony. My host was visibly shocked.

"My friend," I said. "I did that on purpose, to teach you a lesson and make you re-examine your life. Let's look at what ceremonial washing really means. It is an outward symbol of inward purification from the contamination and guilt of sin. You Spiritual Ones take great care to wash the outside of your cups and plates, but inside, your hearts are full of violence and robbery. You think up evil plans that hurt many people on a daily basis. You are such fools! Didn't God, who created your skin that you wash on the outside, also create your hearts on the inside?

"On the one hand, you are all very legalistic in your observance of God's ritual laws. You take one tenth of absolutely everything, even down to your garden herbs, like the sweet-smelling mint, and the leafy rue, and offer it to God in the temple. Yet on the other hand, you completely overlook the fact that God sees the sin that is hidden in your hearts and judges you based on how you treat others!

"I'm not saying that you should neglect tithing. Not at all. You should give God back a tenth of all he gives you. But you should be just as careful to do the right thing and be compassionate to the people around you.

"Let's look at how you treat people. You love to be seen in the most prominent seats in the religious services and you love to shake hands with everyone in the street markets. Watch out, you scheming religious lawyers! You are supposed to be experts in the holy books of God. Watch out, you Spiritual Ones! You are supposed to be examples of true spirituality, but you are such hypocrites!

"You walk around like Greek actors who put on different masks, depending on the character they are playing at any given moment. You live impressive but counterfeit lives and you flatter people to get them to do whatever you want by faking different personalities. People trust you because of your religious titles, but the whole time you are manipulating them with your deadly schemes. It's as if you dug open graves and planned for them to fall in!"[228]

One of the religious experts interrupted me:

"Sir, by saying what you just said about the Spiritual Ones, you are scolding and abusing us as well!"

"You're absolutely right!" I said. "Those of you who are professors and lawyers of religion, you need to look yourselves in the mirror too. You talk big and load people down with so many do's and don'ts and so much responsibility. You put a huge load of spiritual anxiety on their backs. And yet you yourselves won't even touch that load with one of your fingers, much less pick it up and carry it!

"But don't worry. Your judgment is coming too! You donate money to build elaborate monuments and tombstones over the graves of the ancient prophets, without acknowledging that it was your ancestors who murdered those prophets. You are just like them in your attitudes and your actions. In fact, by building these monuments, you are actually showing your support of your wicked ancestors!

"God sent you the prophets to preach his message, knowing full well that some of them would be persecuted and some would be killed, and they were! Their murders will not go un-punished. In fact, it is your generation that will be held responsible for the blood of all the prophets who were murdered since the beginning of time, starting with Abel, the son of Adam and Eve, who was murdered by his brother Cain in an open field;[229] and ending with Zacharias, the priest, who was stoned to death in the temple courtyard on the order of the king.[230]

"Mark my words," I warned my host and his friends sternly. "You will personally pay with your blood for what has happened to the prophets of God over the centuries." They looked at me in disbelief, not realizing that just a few decades in the future, the Romans would totally destroy Jerusalem and kill thousands of our people.

"Watch out, you religious lawyers and so-called experts in the holy books!" I said sternly. "You have actually hidden the key to knowledge and wisdom! You yourselves have no idea how to live a life of freedom and joy. Yet whenever someone else wants to be happy and obey the words of the holy books, you want to tell them how it's done!

"You are legalistic and judgmental in your interpretation of the scriptures. You hinder the people who are trying to experience God's supernatural life by being critical of them," I said. They had nothing more to say after that, and the evening ended quietly.

Not many days after that, a delegation of Spiritual Ones and religious teachers sailed all the way to Capernaum from Jerusalem to question me further. They, too, wanted to know why I allowed my followers to touch food with dirty hands. They had seen some of my team members eating a loaf of bread without first washing their hands and they were shocked.

"Why do your people not follow the customs of our elders?" they asked. "We didn't see them wash their hands before they touched their food!"

"That's a good question," I replied. "But what I want to know is why you Spiritual Ones break the commandments of God and follow your own traditions instead of obeying God's laws?"

Clean Body Or Pure Heart?

The men were shocked and outraged that I would embarrass them in public.

"You Spiritual Ones are such hypocrites!" I said. "You're just like the people in the days of the prophets. You talk nicely to my face and honor me with your lips, but in your hearts you find plenty of reasons to criticize me![231] You passionately express your love for God outwardly; but inwardly, you are basically selfish, going after your own desires and doing whatever suits you best![232]

"Listen carefully to what I have to say," I said, calling the crowds close so they could also hear. "As religious leaders, you Spiritual Ones are wasting your time worshipping God. You may be giving him lip service, but you are not doing what he says! You choose to ignore his commandments and focus instead on keeping up with your own man-made traditions. Instead of being examples of spiritual leadership, you officially teach rules and regulations made up by men just like you!"

"This is outrageous!" the Spiritual Ones were thinking to themselves. *"Now he is really meddling!"*

"Let me give you an example," I said, undeterred by their attitude. "You know that one of the Ten Commandments that Moses brought down from Mt. Sinai is that you should honor your father and your mother. This commandment even has a promise: if you are respectful to your parents, you will live a long life and things will go well for you.[233] If, on the other hand, you curse your parents, you will be stoned to death.[234]

"But you're not worried about that! Instead, you say: 'Mother, Father, I know I should support you financially in your old age. I have some money, but I'm spiritual! So I'm going to give it to the temple as a special gift to God! I know you'll understand!'

"You believe that because you are religious, you can just forget about taking care of your parents and walk away from your responsibilities with a clear conscience! You are supposed to set the example for your people, but you don't. In fact, you conveniently forget to remind them about their financial obligation to their parents, if it means that their money will go to the temple! You are so busy focusing on your own ceremonial washing that you forget to teach them about loving the very people who gave them life!

"You are so busy being right, that you have cut the commands of God right out of your lives. Do you think that your traditions can cancel out God's words and release you from your obligations to take care of your family? This is just one example of your hypocrisy—but believe me, there are many others!

"So let's go back to your question about eating without washing first. Let me make things really clear. There is absolutely nothing that you can put in your mouth that can possibly pollute you! It's what comes out of your mouth that pollutes you! But there's no point in your wasting your time listening to me if you're not going to take my words to heart and apply them in your lives!"

Even though more and more people were gathering to hear what I had to say, I got up and went back inside the house. My team members followed me. Once we were safely inside, Peter cornered me.

"Sir," he said, "how can you say that food can't pollute us? Doesn't God's law clearly list which animals we can eat, and which ones are forbidden?" [235]

Clean Body Or Pure Heart?

"Are you that blind?" I exclaimed. "Don't you see that whatever you put into your mouth can't possibly pollute you, even if you haven't washed your hands? That's because food doesn't go into your heart and mind and affect your behavior. It simply goes into your stomach, where it is digested and eventually expelled from your body and flushed away, making all foods clean.

"It's what comes out of your mouth that actually pollutes you, because it comes straight from your heart. I'm talking about things such as evil thoughts, adultery and all kinds of sexual sins, murder, theft, greed, wickedness, deceit, wild pleasures, the enjoyment of planning evil and doing evil, slander, lying, pride and foolishness. All these terrible things come from deep inside you. They are the real way that you pollute yourselves. It's not eating with unwashed hands! That doesn't pollute your behavior.

"Just know that God sees your hearts, and he knows that since the beginning of time men's thoughts and fantasies have been continually evil from their youth,[236] because the human heart is deceitful above all things, and desperately wicked."[237]

"But what about the Spiritual Ones?" interrupted one of my followers. "Didn't you notice how offended they were by what you told them?" My team members obviously weren't ready to look in their own hearts; they were too busy criticizing others, and worrying about what others thought of them.

"Don't worry about the Spiritual Ones," I said. "They are blind leaders trying to lead a group of blind followers! If the blind lead the blind, they'll both fall into the ditch! As the prophet Isaiah said, their leaders cause them to get off track. They stagger around, not seeing what they are doing, and are themselves destroyed!²³⁸ Leave them alone. Like I said before, every plant that my heavenly father hasn't planted will eventually be pulled up by its roots and thrown into the fire. Let them be. Their day of judgment will come!"

59

Persistence Pays Off

I KNEW AT THAT POINT that the religious lawyers and Spiritual Ones were definitely plotting to kill me. They had sent a clever delegation of spies all the way from Jerusalem to goad me into saying something wrong so they could legally accuse me of a religious crime. I had been very blunt with them, and they were furious. I knew that as soon as they returned to the holy city, they would go straight to the religious leaders to report our conversation. Because of this, I decided not to go south to Jerusalem. I focused instead on traveling around the northern part of the country.

As we made our way west towards the Mediterranean Sea, our journey took us through miles of beautiful vineyards and past groves of lemon and orange trees. We headed towards the coastal towns of Tyre and Sidon, now in modern Lebanon. These cities had a reputation for wickedness.

I didn't want anyone to spot us, so when we came to the outskirts of Tyre, we slipped into the house of some friends. However, one of the servants must have let the word out, because it wasn't long before a local woman came rushing into the house and fell at my feet, crying. She was half-Syrian and half-Palestinian.

"Please help me, Sir," she wailed in Greek, the commercial language of the area. "Help me, Son of David. My daughter is seriously possessed! She is tormented! Please help me, I beg you, and get these demons out of her!"

I didn't say a word. In fact, my team members urged me to send the woman away because she was making so much noise.

"I'm on a mission to the lost sheep among the Hebrew people," I protested, "and you are not a Hebrew!"

"Please help me!" the woman begged, adoringly. "I know you can do it!"

"Let the children of Israel eat first," I said, "because it's not appropriate to take the children's bread and throw it to pagan dogs."

"You're right, Sir," said the woman. "But even the dogs can eat the children's crumbs which fall from their father's table!"

"I'm impressed," I said. "You have great faith. You're not just willing for something good to happen to you. You are assertive. You demand action, and you don't give up till you get what you want! All right, then; you can have what you want! It's yours, because of what you have said. Go home. The devil has gone out of your daughter!"

Sure enough, the woman hurried home and found that the devil was gone, and her daughter was resting calmly on the couch. She had been healed at the exact time of her mother's conversation with me.

We left Tyre and made our way back towards the boomtowns of the Decapolis area on the shores of Lake Galilee, where the freed wild man was now living a productive life. We climbed one of the hilltops overlooking the lake and I sat down to teach again. As usual, huge crowds gathered, bringing their loved ones who were sick, and setting them at my feet with great hope.

Persistence Pays Off

Many of them had heard the story of the two thousand pigs and they were thrilled that I was back in their area.

Some of the patients were crippled and couldn't walk; others were blind; some were deaf; some were unable to speak. There were people who had been injured in accidents; there were some who had been sick or handicapped for years. I healed all of them.

One man arrived, just grunting. He was deaf and had a serious speech impediment. He couldn't talk normally.

"Kind Teacher," the man's relatives begged, "please touch our son and heal him so he can hear and speak like a normal person!"

I took the man aside so we could have some privacy. On an impulse, I put my fingers into his ears. Then I took some of my spit and put it on his tongue. I looked up towards heaven and sighed. Then I spoke to the man's ears and said:

"Ears, open up!"

Immediately, the man's ears popped open and he was able to hear. At the same time, the small piece of skin under his tongue, which had held it tied back and prevented him from speaking clearly, was released. Instantly his speech became normal.

"Jesus is doing everything right!" the people exclaimed. "He's making the deaf hear and the mute speak! We knew he must be special when he freed the wild man. Now he is back and willing to help everyone!"

"Don't tell anyone what you have seen here today," I warned the people; but the more I insisted on their silence, the more they spoke out! They were absolutely amazed at what I was doing. They had personally witnessed the blind see, the lame walk and the mute speak, and they thanked God for it.

Many of them were familiar with the words of the prophet Isaiah, who wrote that the Savior would open the eyes of the blind and unstop the ears of the deaf; the lame would skip like the antelope and the mute would sing for joy![239] As the people meditated on these well-known promises, they were full of wonder and asked themselves if I was indeed the expected one who would save them all.

60

Conflicting Messages

I TAUGHT FOR SEVERAL DAYS in a row, and each day, more people arrived to join the crowds. One day I told them another story:

"God's spiritual community is like a farmer who planted good seeds of wheat in his field. But while everyone was asleep, his enemy came and scattered bad seeds of weeds throughout his wheat field and took off. When blades of wheat started to spring up and develop fruit, the weeds also began to appear, and they grew steadily, mixed in with the wheat.

"One day, the man's loyal slaves came to him and asked:

'Sir, didn't you sow wheat in your field? Where did all these weeds come from?'

'An enemy has done this,' the farmer replied.

'Would you like us to go out there and pull out all the weeds?' asked the slaves.

'No, don't do that,' said the farmer, 'because you might accidentally pull up the wheat with it. Leave everything alone and let them grow up together until it's time for the harvest. At that point, I'll instruct the harvesters to first gather up the weeds and tie them into bundles and burn them. Then they'll gather up the wheat and carry it into my storage barn.'"

Later, when I was alone with my closest team members, I took time to explain the meaning of this story.

"I am the farmer who sows the good seeds, which are God's words. Like sperm, the words contain all the ingredients necessary to create new life in the form of God's spiritual children. The field represents the world. The good seeds grow up to be the children of God, who inherit all the good characteristics of God's personality.

"At the same time, the weeds grow up to be the children of Satan, the wicked one. They inherit all the evil characteristics of Satan's personality. The enemy that sows the weeds is the devil, whose nature it is to bring division without any good reason. The harvest is the end of the world, and the harvesters are the angels.

"Just as weeds are gathered up and burned in the fire, so wicked people will be separated out at the end of the world. I will send out my angels to pick up all the people who are offensive to God and who disregard his laws. The angels will grab them and throw them into the fires of hell, where they will scream forever, bitterly regretting all the bad things they have done!

"Once the wicked people are out of the way, those who are related to God by love will shine in their father's community as brightly as the stars in heaven. They are the people who live in a personal relationship with God and conform to his standards. So if you hear my words, pay close attention to what I'm saying."

The people were hungry for my teachings and they refused to leave. I had been teaching for three days, and they were still standing there listening to me. By this time, most of them had run out of food. I took a break from teaching and called my team members together.

"I feel really sorry for these people!" I said. "They've been standing here listening to me for three days and they have nothing left to eat. I don't want to send them home without first feeding them. Many have come from quite far away. They are too weak and might collapse if they had to walk all the way back on an empty stomach!"

"Where do you expect us to find enough food to feed such a large crowd?" asked my team members, obviously forgetting the miraculous feeding of the five thousand people just days before! "How can we possibly satisfy all these people here in the middle of nowhere?" they protested.

"How many loaves of bread do you have this time?" I asked.

"We've got seven loaves of bread and a few small fish," they said.

I told the crowds to just sit down on the ground and relax. Then I picked up the seven loaves and blessed them. I broke the bread in pieces and gave it to my team members to serve the people, which they did.

Then I picked up the basket of fish, blessed it and asked my helpers to distribute them also. Everyone ate until they were full. Then we gathered up all the leftovers and they filled seven baskets. Approximately four thousand men were fed this time, not counting the women and children.

Then I sent them all home.

61

Religious People Can Be Hypocrites

WE LEFT THE TEN TOWNS of the Decapolis and sailed towards Dalmanutha on the west coast of the lake, just a few miles north of Herod's shiny new capital, Tiberias. Nearby was the little town of Magdala, the home town of Mary Magdalene. She was so grateful for being set free from the demons that had controlled her life that she traveled with us and served us daily. She was standing on deck, eager to be back in her home town, when we docked.

As soon as I got off the boat, however, the local Spiritual Ones and the Realists came down to the harbor to give me a hard time. They knew that Mary Magdalene was traveling with our group and they were resentful.

"Teacher," they said, "we challenge you to produce a sign from heaven to prove that you have the power of God!" They were pretending to be sincere, but in their hearts they were mean. They were determined to do everything they could legally do to find some weakness or evil in me so they could arrest me.

I was really disappointed to see what they were doing.

"Why do you people keep wanting to see a sign?" I sighed. "I'm not going to give you one. You already know what is going on.

"When you see that the sky is red in the evening, you know that the weather will be nice the following morning; and when you see that the sky is red and overcast in the morning, you know that it will be a stormy day. Don't tell me that you can look at the sky and see what it's telling you, yet when you see my miracles, you suddenly act stupid, and don't know what they mean! You are such hypocrites! Such great actors! As I've said before, people who are into magic and who cheat on their wives want signs, but the only sign you will get is the sign of the prophet Jonah!"

With that, I got back into the boat and we sailed off to the other side of Lake Galilee. Mary Magdalene was dismayed at the attitude of her townspeople and had no regrets about having left her home town to travel with us. When we landed on the opposite coast, my team members were in a panic.

"We forgot to bring food! All we have in the boat is one loaf of bread!" one of them said.

"That reminds me," I answered, "you need to be on the lookout for yeast among the Spiritual Ones and the Realists, and especially in Governor Herod Antipas. His yeast is fermenting in the heat of current circumstances and it is about to rise to the explosion point. We are heading into a major political crisis!"

My team members didn't understand what I was talking about. They argued amongst themselves and decided that I was probably referring to the fact that they hadn't brought enough bread.

"Why are you fighting over the fact that you don't have enough bread?" I asked, knowing what they were really thinking. "You assume that I'm talking about yeast because we're out of bread, don't you? You have no clue what I'm talking about, do you? Are you as hard-headed as the leaders of Magdala? You have eyes, but you obviously can't see me. You have ears, but you obviously can't hear me.

"What little faith you have! You were there when I fed the five thousand men with only five loaves of bread, weren't you? How many baskets of leftovers did you collect that day?"

"Twelve," they said sheepishly.

"And you saw me feed four thousand men with seven loaves of bread, didn't you? How many baskets of leftovers did you collect that day?"

"Seven," they answered.

"So, having experienced both of those miracles, how is it that you don't understand that I'm not talking about literal loaves of bread and literal yeast? I'm talking about the hidden hypocrisy of the Spiritual Ones and the Realists. You saw how they treated me in Magdala. Well, worse is yet to come!"

Then they understood that I was not warning them about the yeast in bread, but about the hypocritical beliefs and teachings of the religious groups.

62

Finally Somebody Gets It!

SOON AFTER THAT, I TOOK my followers back to the retreat in Bethsaida to try and have some time alone to relax. It wasn't long before crowds gathered again, bringing a blind man to see me.

"Please touch him and heal him!" they begged.

I grabbed the blind man by the arm and led him outside the city limits. Taking some of my spit, I put it on his eyelids and then I told him to open his eyes.

"Can you see anything?" I asked. The man strained to see what he could see.

"I can see people," he said, "but they're out of focus! They look kinda' like trees walking!"

I touched his eyes one more time.

"All right; now take another look," I said.

"Wow! I can see clearly now!" the man exclaimed. "Everything is in perfect focus!"

"I want you to go straight home," I told him. "Don't go back into town, and don't tell anyone what just happened here. Just go home!"

From Bethsaida we went from village to village along the lake shore and ended up at a beautiful ancient town called Caesarea Philippi, on the hilly slopes of snow-covered Mt. Hermon.

The Roman Emperor, Caesar Augustus, had given this town to Herod the Great, who had built an impressive Roman temple there. Later, his son, Philip, Herodias's ex-husband, expanded the city with beautiful new buildings that glistened in the sun as we walked by.

One morning, I got up early as usual. After spending some time in prayer, I took my team on a leisurely walk along the country road. It was time to find out what they really believed about me. They had been with me for about three years now. I wanted to see what they had learned, and if they were ready for me to make what was to be my final trip to Jerusalem.

"Who do people say that I am?" I asked. They all had different answers:

"Some believe what Governor Herod is saying—that you're John the Baptist come back from the dead!"

"Some say you're the re-incarnation of the prophet Elijah who went off to heaven in a chariot!"

"A lot of people think you're Jeremiah, or some ancient prophet come back to life!"

"And what about you? Who do you think I am?" I asked them.

Peter didn't hesitate:

"You're the Savior we've all been waiting for!" he exclaimed. "It's clear that you've been chosen and set apart by God to be our High Priest and our Savior. I'm convinced that you are the Son of the true and living God!"

"Simon Peter, son of Jonas," I said, "you got it! You recognize who I am. God has allowed you to see something that was previously unknown to man. He has shown you who I am by giving

Finally Somebody Gets It!

you a supernatural revelation of the truth. You're blessed. What you have just confessed proves that God truly lives in you!

"Since your name, Peter, means 'a rock', I'm going to build God's whole spiritual community on you and on the truth of what you just said. God's community will stand firm. Nothing will ever be strong enough to overpower it—not even the gates of hell itself! What's more, I will give you the keys to that spiritual community.

"Whatever you declare to be binding on earth will be considered binding by heaven. Whatever you pronounce as abolished on earth will be considered abolished by heaven. As for the rest of you, I'm instructing you not to tell anyone that I am the Savior. Please keep this secret knowledge to yourselves."

This conversation was the high point of almost three years of training. After being with me day and night—watching me, listening to me—finally, one of them actually understood who I really was! I wouldn't have to keep explaining it any more. Peter got it!

Peter recognized who I was. He realized that I really was the long-awaited Savior, and he had put it into words in front of the group!

That's when I knew it was time to move on. It was time to let my closest friends and followers know exactly what the rest of God's plan for my mission involved, and what lay ahead for me. I gathered them all together and sat down to make an important announcement.

"I want you all to pay careful attention. I have some really important news to share with you," I told them. They looked at me with great expectation, wondering what was so important. I had never made an announcement before.

"It's time for me to go to Jerusalem," I said. "I know you have tried to stop me, but there is no stopping me now. I have to move forward and complete my mission. I know that when I get to Jerusalem, I will have to endure incredible pain and suffering. I want to tell you exactly what is going to happen, so you can be prepared.

"First, the respected religious elders, chief priests and religious professors will turn on me. They represent the people, and their decisions are final. They are determined to have me killed, and I will let them."

Everyone looked stunned. What was I saying? They tried to understand.

"Yes, I will die a horrible death, just like the prophets have written. But that's not the end of the story. Even though I will be dead and buried, on day three, I will come back to life."

They gasped, looking at me for an explanation. Nothing I was saying made any sense to them. I could tell that they loved me and they didn't want to let me suffer.

"I know you're shocked," I said, "but I'm warning you now, so that you may recognize it when it happens and not be surprised."

Peter didn't like what I was saying at all. He took me aside privately and began to scold me for being so negative.

"God is a good God," he whispered, so that the others wouldn't hear. "He won't let you down. These terrible things can never happen to you! You don't deserve to suffer. Just don't go to Jerusalem and you can avoid all this!"

His words had absolutely no effect on me. On the contrary, I reprimanded him.

Finally Somebody Gets It!

"Stop it, Peter!" I said. "You're the voice of the devil when you talk like that, and I refuse to listen to you! Your protests are offensive to me! You're thinking like a man—instead of flowing in the things of God!

"Do you remember how King David called Zeruiah 'Satan' when he opposed David's wishes?[240] Well, I'm calling you 'Satan' right now. You're going directly against my wishes. You are acting like a stumbling block and trying to stop me from doing what I have to do!"

I called the rest of the team back, and they crowded around to listen.

"Let me make things crystal clear," I said. "If you really want to follow me, you have to stop focusing on yourselves and on your own personal agendas! Instead, you must publicly serve your own death sentence by picking up your cross daily.

"This means that you have to crucify your own plans and focus on mine. You have to give up all of your own personal needs and wants on a daily basis. If necessary, you must even be willing to accept deep shame and humiliation because of me. Only when you are prepared to live like that are you ready to walk through life by my side. That's what it really means to follow me!

"If you try to hold onto your own life, and try to do it all your own way, you'll end up wrecking your life, or losing it. But if you voluntarily kill your own future, and give up living for yourself to live for me and for the good news of God's salvation, you'll actually end up saving your soul!

"Do you have any idea what your soul is worth? If you were to buy up the whole world and everything in it, but traded in your own soul as payment, what good would that do you? Once you've lost your soul, there isn't enough money in the universe to buy it back again!" I explained.

"The holy books say that even if you were extremely wealthy and boasted about all your riches, you could never buy eternal freedom for your friends and relatives; nor could you ever pay God enough ransom money to buy back their souls. You can't even put a price to a soul, because your soul—the real you—lives forever. And how can you put a value on you?[241] You're priceless!

"My words may be tough and my standards high, but this is it! If you're ashamed of me and my words here on Earth, then one day I will be ashamed of you.

"You may be embarrassed to be seen as my followers when you are around unbelievers and habitual sinners, who waste their lives away by flirting with anyone and anything instead of putting me first. If you are, when I come back to earth in my glory and in the splendor of my father, accompanied by hosts of glistening angels, then I will be embarrassed to be seen with you!" I said.

"I have made God's will very clear to each and every one of you," I continued. "It's up to you now to decide what kind of life you choose to live. Only you can decide whether or not you will follow me.

"As for me—my mind is made up!

"I have to keep walking till I get to Jerusalem …"

To be continued...

For the rest of the story, order:

"The Week That Changed The World"

by Helen Hunter

JOIN THE MOVEMENT

Everyone around the globe knows about Coca Cola. Everyone - even in the poorest villages - has a cell phone. But not everyone has heard of Jesus.

At the same time, almost 10,000 people a day Google: Who is Jesus? If you give them a Bible, it's like handing them an encyclopedia. They don't know where to begin! But if you give them a copy of the book **The Jesus Diaries** they will fall in love with Jesus and RUN to the Bible.

If you are one of the millions who wants to share the good news about Jesus with others, but you don't know where to start - just read the book and share it with your friends and family in person or on Facebook or Twitter...

Together, we can reach the world!

MEET HELEN HUNTER

Helen Hunter is a dynamic and inspirational speaker, radio personality and author of historical fiction books. The Number One comment people make about her books is:

"I couldn't put it down!"

The eldest child of Czech refugees who fled Communism to the British Isles, Helen was educated in universities in Scotland, Belgium, Mexico and the United States. She is fluent in several languages, and has a degree as a simultaneous interpreter and translator in English, Spanish and French.

For over forty years, Helen has been a diligent student of the Bible. She attended seminary and graduate school of theology. She has studied biblical Hebrew and Greek and has read the Bible through from cover to cover in English, French and Spanish.

Helen has traveled and ministered extensively in over 100 countries around the world, including Israel, Egypt and Jordan. She has interviewed people from all walks of life, from tribesmen in Africa to business leaders in China.

As an international communicator—a teacher in Africa, an interpreter in Europe, a radio reporter in Asia, a conference speaker in Latin America and a motivational speaker in the United States—Helen has a unique global perspective. She brings her cultural insights and profound understanding of people into her fascinating and inspirational books and speeches, and makes the places she writes about come to life.

You feel you are right there with her—hunting with the Pygmies, living in a native village in Mexico, eating off a banana leaf with an Indian Sikh in Kuala Lumpur, standing on a street corner in Jerusalem...

Her life of extraordinary adventure and opportunity has provided Helen with exciting material from exotic places to use in her books and speeches. At the same time, as a refugee, she has had her fair share of tough times with the loss of relationships, physical and emotional health, property and finances.

On a deeper level, it has been in the times of struggle that she gained compassion for others, insight into healing and recovery, and the ability to use each breakdown as an opportunity for a breakthrough to a higher level.

Helen owns her own consulting and management firm, which she has led for over twenty years. She has an extraordinary grasp of the cultural and economic dynamics of our changing world and speaks with insight, conviction and charm.

WHAT AUDIENCES ARE SAYING:

"Mesmerizing speaker, life-changing message, powerful delivery."

"Helen tells a story like nobody I've ever heard before."

"Colorful, delivered with style and wit! She's like a human billboard."

Meet Helen Hunter

"Helen has tremendous breadth of experience and fantastic articulation."

"Terrific on-point analysis…"

"Exciting! I kept wanting to know how it ended. Marvelous vocal variety and gestures."

"Helen Hunter has a way of reaching people with great clarity."

"I could picture it all—I felt like I was right there…"

"The fullness of her subject matter is terrific. It makes me interested in finding out more."

For more information about Helen Hunter
and her other books, visit:

www.HelenHunterInternational.com

BACK STORY
Interview with author, Helen Hunter

Why did you write *The Jesus Diaries?*

Like many small children in Christian lands, I grew up hearing stories about Jesus - how he was born in a manger in Bethlehem, how he loved little children, how he healed people and did many wonderful miracles. The stories were sweet, but as I grew older, they were no longer relevant to my daily life. Like Snow White and the Seven Dwarfs, and Hansel and Gretel, Jesus in a manger seemed to be just a fairy tale.

As I grew a little older, I started hearing more about Jesus dying on a cross for the sins of the world. Whenever I visited different churches and cathedrals in Europe, I would be in awe of their beautiful stained glass windows and amazing gothic arches - until I would come upon a grotesque and disgusting sight. There, usually in a little nook near the entrance, I would find a horrific porcelain statue of Jesus half naked, with a cut in his side, a crown of thorns on his head, and blood dripping down his anguished face. It was revolting and I did not like to look at it.

In high school we learned about the historical Jesus. He was more than the sweet stories from my childhood. We read the actual facts about his life from the gospel texts. The more I studied the gospels, the more confused I became.

First of all, the life of Jesus was recounted in four different versions, in Matthew, Mark, Luke and John. Some of the stories overlapped, some were completely different. Each version

Back Story

seemed to focus on a different aspect of his character, but there was nowhere I could go and read one continuous version that had everything in it.

Secondly, Jesus' words were like riddles and I didn't understand what they meant. At school, the teacher would spend lesson after lesson explaining to us what the customs of his day were, so we could understand what he was referring to - but his words still made no sense. I was intrigued, challenged, fascinated and perplexed.

Finally, I realized that the most famous sayings of Jesus had become so familiar, that they no longer had any impact. They were beautiful words that sounded good; poetic words that were nostalgic, but powerless. I had become so attached to the tradition of hearing the words themselves, that I no longer paid attention to their actual meaning. Worse yet, it felt almost sacrilegious to question those famous words and try to understand what they really meant. That's when I had to remind myself that the words I was so attached to were not even his original words - they were a translation!

Obviously, Jesus had an incredible impact on the history of the western world and on the beliefs and behavior of countless millions of people throughout the world. If that was the case - why could I not just simply open a book and read about his life and his teachings and understand his words right away?

How did you go about writing it?

I decided to go to seminary and discovered a book called *A Harmony of the Gospels*. Now, I could take the gospel texts and study them side by side, but that still didn't solve my problem. It was like working on a math puzzle - not meeting a person. I still had to work with disjointed information, which made getting to know Jesus very unnatural and unmanageable.

I also learned that others as far back as the second century had merged the gospel texts, consolidating all the information into one narrative, so I bought an amalgamated version of the texts. That helped, but it still didn't come alive for me.

So I decided that maybe if I studied one of the ancient languages, I would understand Jesus better. I already had a degree as an interpreter and translator, so I took a year at Masters level and studied biblical Hebrew. I also studied biblical Greek. All that proved to me was that the many translations we already have are excellent and that they tell us exactly what the ancient texts say.

So now what? I still didn't have a user-friendly way to study Jesus' life and teachings from the source. What should I do? Oh, I believed. I had a personal relationship with Jesus. I heard sermons and meditations about Jesus. But it wasn't enough. If I was going to go higher in my relationship with God, I was determined to squeeze the information out of the actual gospel texts and find out exactly what they said. I was not satisfied with having second-hand knowledge and listening to others tell me what they saw in the texts. I was determined to crack open their secrets myself.

Furthermore, I was sure that if I was frustrated after having put out such great effort to get to know Jesus, that there were probably many others who felt the same way. As I talked to different people about the problem, I found that they we were resigned about the situation and didn't expect anything more. But I did. I was determined to really get to know what the texts were all about.

To do that, I bought a book called *The Hebrew-Greek Study Bible*. Every day, I would read a few verses and look up the meaning of every word. Then I would track back to the Old Testament references and study the background of the culture and the context of the stories.

That's when things turned around. What I realized was, that without thoroughly understanding the world of the Old Testament, it was impossible to understand Jesus. Jesus came to fulfill the writings of the ancient prophets. So if I didn't understand what the prophets were saying, and why they believed what they believed, I could not possibly understand what Jesus was saying. And if I didn't understand how the ancient Hebrews lived on a daily basis, and what they believed to be true in their lives, I couldn't possibly understand Jesus either.

That's when it really got interesting. As I delved into the Old Testament context for each of Jesus' teachings, and the exact meaning of the words he used, his words suddenly became crystal clear. I could picture it all, just like he saw it.

And that's when I had the idea of telling his story through his eyes, simply by turning the text from third to first person. Instead of writing "Jesus saw the blind man and said..." for example, I wrote "I saw the blind man and said..." Wow! That was really exciting. Getting inside Jesus' life and actually going through it with him, looking with his eyes, hearing with his ears... that really made it come alive - just by changing the grammatical point of view from "he" to "I".

By now, I was on a roll. I wanted to know what the scenery was like as he was walking along. I went to Israel, Egypt and Jordan and took a good look around. I also began to research more specific information about the crops that grew along the roads he walked, the background of the people he interacted with - and before you know it, *The Jesus Diaries* became a reality!

How do we know that the book is scripturally sound?
That's a great question. I realized that church leaders would want to make sure that the book is accurate. So I asked Professor James R. Adair, a seasoned Bible scholar who taught at several universities in the United States and abroad, and author of the best history of Christianity I have ever read, called **Introducing Christianity,** to read *The Jesus Diaries* with a fine tooth comb. He made some editing suggestions and corrected a few minor points, which I really appreciate and which make me feel very confident in recommending this book to the academic community.

ENDNOTES

The following references may be found in any version of the Bible.

1. Joshua 21:9-11.
2. 1 Chronicles 24:19.
3. 1 Chronicles 23:13.
4. Ezra 30:7,8.
5. Ezra 27:20-21.
6. Leviticus 16:2.
7. Judges 6:22.
8. Daniel 10:8.
9. Numbers 6:3-6.
10. Judges 13:5.
11. 1 Samuel 1:11.
12. Malachi 4:5,6.
13. Daniel 8:16.
14. Ezekiel 3:26.
15. Ezekiel 24:27.
16. Numbers 6:24-26.
17. Genesis 30:23.
18. Daniel 9:21-23.
19. Isaiah 7:14,15.
20. Psalms 138:6.
21. Leviticus 12:3.
22. Genesis 17:12.
23. Exodus 4:31.
24. Genesis 22:16,17.
25. Genesis 17:4.
26. Genesis 12:3.
27. Malachi 3:1.
28. Isaiah 40:3.
29. Psalms 145:8,9.
30. Zechariah 3:8.
31. Zechariah 6:12.
32. Isaiah 11:1-4.
33. Malachi 4:2.
34. Isaiah 9:2.
35. Isaiah 42:7.
36. Isaiah 49:9.
37. Deuteronomy 24:1.
38. Deuteronomy 22:22.
39. Isaiah 7:14.
40. Isaiah 9:6,7.
41. Genesis 28:12.
42. Genesis 32:1,2.
43. Exodus 34: 28-30.
44. Psalms 103:20,21.
45. Daniel 7:10.
46. Genesis 37:11.
47. Leviticus 12:2-6.
48. Exodus 13:2.
49. Numbers 18:15.
50. Deuteronomy. 21:15-17.
51. Leviticus 12:2.
52. Isaiah 40:1.
53. Isaiah 60:1-3.
54. Isaiah 9:2.
55. Numbers 6:25.
56. Isaiah 52:10.
57. Isaiah 49:6.
58. Isaiah 8:14.
59. Hosea 14:9.
60. Numbers 24:17.
61. Micah 5:2.
62. Genesis 30:1.

63 Genesis 35:19.
64 Psalms 72:10.
65 Isaiah 60:6.
66 Jeremiah 31:15.
67 Hosea 11:1.
68 Deuteronomy 16:16.
69 Exodus 23: 14-17.
70 2 Kings 17:24.
71 Leviticus 12:2-4.
72 Leviticus 11:22.
73 Exodus 3:1-10.
74 Genesis 9:26.
75 2 Kings 1:8.
76 Malachi 4:5.
77 Malachi 4:1.
78 Leviticus 19:11.
79 Exodus 23:1.
80 Malachi 3:1,2.
81 Joel 2:28.
82 Deuteronomy 18:15,18.
83 Isaiah 40:3.
84 Exodus 12:3, 5.
85 Isaiah 53:7.
86 Psalms 2:7.
87 Isaiah 42:1-7.
88 Deuteronomy 8:3.
89 Deuteronomy 6:13.
90 Deuteronomy 10:20.
91 Psalms 9:11,12.
92 Deuteronomy 6:16.
93 Joshua 24:14.
94 Micah 5:2.
95 Psalms 32:2.
96 Psalms 73:1.
97 Genesis 28:12.
98 1 Samuel 16:7.
99 1 Chronicles 28:9.
100 Numbers 21:9.
101 Job 24:13,17.
102 2 Kings 4:33.
103 Ecclesiastes 5:2.
104 1 Kings 8:26-29.
105 Psalms 103:20,21.
106 Proverbs 30:8.
107 Job 23:12.
108 1 Chronicles 29:11.
109 Jeremiah 29:12,13.
110 Proverbs 8:17
111 Malachi 3:1.
112 Leviticus 18:16.
113 Leviticus 20:21.
114 Genesis 33:19.
115 Judges 9:7.
116 2 Kings 17:29.
117 Isaiah 12:3.
118 Isaiah 44:3.
119 Zechariah 13:1.
120 Job 23:12.
121 Daniel 12:3.
122 Deuteronomy 16:16-17.
123 Deuteronomy 6:4.
124 Isaiah 61:1.
125 Psalms 45:2.
126 1 Kings 17:9.
127 2 Kings 5:14.
128 Exodus 20:13.
129 2 Samuel 6:20.
130 Proverbs 25:8.
131 Psalms 32:6
132 Isaiah 55:6.
133 Isaiah 9:2.
134 Isaiah 60:1.
135 Genesis 8:21.
136 Jeremiah 29:11.

Endnotes

137 Leviticus 19:18.
138 Deuteronomy 23:23.
139 Numbers 30:2.
140 Isaiah 53:4.
141 Leviticus 14:3,4,10.
142 Job 14:4.
143 Isaiah 43:25.
144 Isaiah 2:2,3.
145 Hosea 6:6.
146 Isaiah 58:5.
147 Isaiah 58:6,9.
148 Nehemiah 3:1.
149 Exodus 20:10.
150 Jeremiah 17:21-27.
151 Jeremiah 17:21-27.
152 Jeremiah 17:25.
153 Daniel 7:13,14.
154 Isaiah 26:19.
155 Daniel 12:2.
156 Deuteronomy 19:15.
157 Isaiah 8:20.
158 Deuteronomy 18:15,18.
159 Isaiah 8:20.
160 Deuteronomy 23:25
161 1 Samuel 21:6.
162 Exodus 29:32,33.
163 2 Chronicles 6:18.
164 Malachi 3:1.
165 Hosea 6:6.
166 Micah 6:8.
167 Exodus 23:4,5.
168 Isaiah 57:15.
169 Isaiah 61:2,3.
170 Isaiah 55:1.
171 Psalms 41:1.
172 Psalms 91.
173 Psalms 15:2.
174 Psalms 107:20.
175 Isaiah 2:2,3.
176 Malachi 1:11.
177 Isaiah 2:2,3.
178 Genesis 3:19.
179 Genesis 49:10
180 Numbers 24:17.
181 Isaiah 35:4-6.
182 Isaiah 29:18.
183 Isaiah 42:7.
184 Psalms 22:6.
185 Isaiah 61:1.
186 Isaiah 8:14,15.
187 Malachi 3:1.
188 Brad Young. P53.*
189 Micah 2:13.
190 Malachi 4:5,6.
191 Jonah 3:7,8.
192 Isaiah 14:3.
193 Psalms 8:2.
194 Jeremiah 6:16.
195 Psalms 23:5.
196 Exodus 8:19.
197 Daniel 2:44.
198 Jonah 1:17.
199 1 Kings 10:10.
200 1 Kings 10:1.
201 Job 1:7.
202 Isaiah 58:2.
203 Jeremiah 4:3.
204 Psalms 78:2.
205 Proverbs 4:18.
206 Leviticus 15:19-24.
207 1 Kings 17:17-4.
208 2 Kings 4:8-37.
209 Deuteronomy 1:16,17.
210 Psalms 147:9.

[211] Isaiah 9:1.
[212] Numbers 27:17.
[213] Isaiah 53:6.
[214] Ezekiel 34:16.
[215] 1 Samuel 9:7.
[216] 2 Samuel 23:2.
[217] Exodus 4:12.
[218] Exodus 4:12.
[219] Micah 7:6.
[220] Isaiah 8:13,14.
[221] Psalms 55:12-14.
[222] Numbers 11:13.
[223] 2 Kings 4:42-44.
[224] Job 9:8.
[225] Song of Solomon 1:4.
[226] Isaiah 54:13.
[227] Micah 4:2.
[228] Psalms 5:9.
[229] Genesis 4:8
[230] 2 Chronicles 24:20,21.
[231] Isaiah 29:13.
[232] Ezekiel 33:31.
[233] Exodus 20:12.
[234] Exodus 21:17.
[235] Leviticus 11:1-30.
[236] Genesis 6:5.
[237] Jeremiah 17:9.
[238] Isaiah 9:16.
[239] Isaiah 5:5,6.
[240] 2 Samuel 19:22.
[241] Psalms 49:7,8.

* *Jesus The Jewish Theologian,* by Brad H. Young.

Contact Information

For more information about Helen Hunter
and her other books, please visit:

www.HelenHunterInternational.com

Made in the USA
Columbia, SC
11 March 2019